Anonymous

Methodist Tune Book

A collection of tunes adapted to the Methodist hymn book

Anonymous

Methodist Tune Book
A collection of tunes adapted to the Methodist hymn book

ISBN/EAN: 9783337082772

Printed in Europe, USA, Canada, Australia, Japan

Cover: Foto ©Thomas Meinert / pixelio.de

More available books at **www.hansebooks.com**

METHODIST TUNE BOOK.

A COLLECTION

OF

Tunes Adapted to the Methodist Hymn Book.

COMPILED BY A COMMITTEE.

TORONTO:
METHODIST BOOK AND PUBLISHING HOUSE.

HALIFAX:
METHODIST BOOK ROOM.

PREFACE.

AT the request of the Executive of the Western Section of the Book Committee of the Methodist Church of Canada, the Revs. Enoch Wood, D.D., Ephraim B. Harper, D D., Alexander Sutherland, D.D., John A. Williams, D.D., Richard Brown, Esq., J. B. Boustead, Esq., William Cluxton, Esq., and C. W. Coates, Esq., consented to form a Committee to prepare a collection of Tunes suitable to the various metres found in the New Hymn Book. A circular, inviting co-operation, was sent to the ministers, organists, and the principal leaders of choirs throughout the Connexion, which met with a large response; and the compilation now presented to the Church is the result.

The Music has been selected with great care, from the best sources, and with special reference to its adaptability for Congregational use, and at the same time meeting the growing improvement in the service of song observable in most of our Churches.

The Tunes here presented will be found to be in accord with the spirit and character of the Hymns in use amongst us; and the adoption of them, it is hoped, will promote intelligent expression, and devout feeling, in one of the most delightful exercises of Christian worship.

Many of the Tunes have been tested by long usage, and have become sacred as a medium of praise; others are relatively new; yet an acquaintance with them will soon render them as popular as the old.

The Committee express sincere thanks to those Publishers who have kindly permitted their copyright music to be inserted in this collection.

To Her Most Gracious Majesty the Queen, for permission to insert No. 341, a production of H. R. H. the late Prince Consort.

EDITORIAL NOTE.

As most of the tunes are printed in open notes, care should be taken not to sing too slowly. It is a mistake to suppose that all music so written is necessarily slow. For guidance in singing, certain terms are used. "Cheerful," etc., prefixed to the tunes, the terms being supposed to represent the time as marked by the single beat of a pendulum or metronome, as follows :—

Joyful,	Pendulum	22 inches.	Metronome 80 = ♩
Cheerful,	"	27 "	" 72 = ♩
Moderate,	"	31 "	" 66 = ♩
Slowly,	"	38 "	" 60 = ♩
Slow,	"	48 "	" 54 = ♩

In following these indications, it should be remembered that the character of the hymn, the construction of the melody, the size of the congregation, and other circumstances, will be found to exert an influence upon the speed of the music.

INDEX I.—METRICAL.

L. M.

	No.
Albion	1
Angels' Song	2
Bartholdy	3
Carmel	4
Church Triumphant	5
Communion	6
Crasselius	7
Crucifixion	8
Dresden	9
Duke Street	10
Eden	11
Erfurt	12
Ernan	13
Eucharist	14
Evening Hymn	15
Federal Street	16
Fulham	17
Germany	18
Hamburg	19
Hursley	20
Intercession	21
Luton	22
Mainzer	23
Melbourne	24
Melcombe	25
Milton	26
Montgomery	27
Morning Hymn	28
Munich	29
Newcastle	30
Newmarket	31
Norwood	32
Old Hundred	33
Old Saxony	34
Olives' Brow	35
Ossett	36
Overburg	37
Page	38
Pentecost	39
Rockingham	40
Rotherfield	41
Sabbath	42
Sessions	43
Stratham	44
Susannah	45
St. Alban	46
St. Crispin	47
St. Cross	48
St. George	49
St. Olaves	50
St. Sepulchre	51
St. Vincent	52
Turin	53
Truro	54

L. M.—Continued.

	No.
Vespers	55
Ward	56
Warrington	57
Wavertree	58
Windham	59
Worcester	60
Wareham	61

L. M. (Double).

	No.
Sunset	62
St. Serf	63

C.M.

	No.
Abridge	64
Andrews	65
Arnold	66
Ashley	67
Aubery	68
Balerma	69
Bedford	70
Belmont	71
Bristol	72
Caddo	73
Childhood	74
Claremont	75
Coronation (New)	76
Dublin	77
Dundee	78
Eagley	79
Emmanuel	80
Evan	81
Farrant	82
Harrington	83
Hartley	84
Hatfield	85
Holy Cross	86
Holy Trinity	87
Horsley	88
Howard	89
Huddersfield	90
Irish	91
Jazer	92
Kensington	93
Lanesboro'	94
Manchester	95
Martyrdom	96
Messiah	97
Miles' Lane	98
Mirfield	99
Newton	100
Peregrinus	101
Peterborough	102
Prescott	103

C.M.—Continued.

	No.
Rephidim	104
Robbins	105
Rose Hill	106
Rose Lane	107
Salisbury	108
Spohr	109
Southwell	110
St. Agnes	111
St. Ann's	112
St. Bernard	113
St. David	114
St. Fulbert	115
St. Mary's	116
St. Peter	117
St. Stephen	118
Tallis' Ordinal	119
Tottenham	120
Trenton	121
Trinity	122
Walsal	123
Warwick	124
Whitby	125
York	126
Zwingle	127

C.M. (Double).

	No.
Bethlehem	128
Bonar	129
Ellacombe	130
Haydn	131
St. Ursula	132

S.M.

	No.
Bankfield	133
Bethel	134
Boylston	135
Cambridge	136
Cana	137
Carlisle	138
Christ Church	139
Dennis	140
Falcon Street	141
Franconia	142
Leeds	143
Mount Ephraim	144
Potsdam	145
Prague	146
Rhodes	147
Sabbath	148
Sarah	149
Serenity	150
Shirland	151
Supplication	152

S. M.—Continued.

	No.
St. Bride	153
St. Giles	154
St. Helena	155
St. Mary Redcliffe	156
St. Michael	157
Thatcher	158
Tuam	159
Warksworth	160
Whitefield	161

S. M. (Double).

	No.
Armageddon	162
Diademata	163
Leomister	164
Nearer Home	165

8S, 88, 8S.

	No.
Adoration	166
Bremen	167
Brighton	168
Calcutta	169
Castleton	170
Celestis Urbs	171

88, 88, 88.—Continued.

	No.
Colmar	172
Creation	173
Eaton	174
Euphony	175
Giessen	176
Maccabeus	177
Melita	178
Middlesex	179
Stella	180
Swaffham	181
St. Catherine	182
St. Matthias	183
St. Paul	184
St. Werbergh	185
Valete	186

888, 888. (2nd Metre).

	No.
Bradford	187
Brunswick Chapel	188
Centennial	189
Lucerne	190
Monmouth	191
Zurich	192

66, 66, 88.

	No.
Acclamation	193
Bevan	194
Caledon	195
Darwell	196
Jubilee	197
Millennium	198
Penrhyn	199
Samuel	200
Southampton	201
Steggall	202
St. Swithin	203

886, 886.

	No.
Ariel	204
Harwood	205
Inspruck	206
Iona	207
Magdalen College	208
Maudesley Street	209
Meribah	210
Pembroke	211
Purleigh	212

Measure.	Name of Tune.	No.	Measure.	Name of Tune.	No.
5.5.9, 5.5.9.	Hungerford	213	7.6, 7.6, 7.6, 7.6	Lancashire	243
	Stour Valley	214		Missionary	244
5.5.11, 5.5.11.	Harwich	215		Morning Light	245
5.5.5, 11	Derbe	216		Rutherford	246
	Sherbrook	217		St. Theodulph	247
6.4, 6.4, 6.6.4	Bethany	218	7.6, 7.6, 7.7, 7.6	Asylum	248
	Love	219		Cowley	249
	Sullivan	220		Faith	250
6.5, 6.5, 6.5, 6.5.	Onward	221		Galt	251
6.6.4, 6.6.4	"Lowly and Solemn be"	222		St. Hilary	252
6.6.4, 6 6.6.4	Canada	223	7.6, 7.6, 7.8, 7.6	Amsterdam	253
	God Save the Queen	224		Falkirk	254
	Italian Hymn	225		Gilead	255
	Newhaven	226		Josiah	256
	Olivet	227	7 6, 7.6, 8.8	Russ-ll Place	257
6.6, 6.6.	Fiducia	228		St. Antolius	258
6.6, 6.6, 6.6.	Lomas	229	7.7.7	Twilight	259
6.6, 6.6, 6.6, 6.6.	Sheba	230		Comfort	260
6.6, 7.7, 7.7	Eccles	231		St. Philip	261
	Fulneck	232	7.7.7.7	Ascension	262
	Thornton	233		Ashford	263
6.6.8, 6.6.8.	Crusader's Hymn	234		Christ Chapel	264
	Hilary	235		Clarion	265
	Jerusalem	236		Easter Hymn	266
6.6.8.4, 6.6.8.4	Harvington	237		Essex	267
	Leoni	238		German Hymn	268
6.6.8, 6.8.8	Bath	239		Harrow	269
	Lucca	240		Holley	270
7.6, 7.6, 7.6, 7.6	Aurelia	241		Innocents	271
	Ewing	242		Judah	272
				Mariner's	273

Measure.	Name of Tune.	No.	Measure.	Name of Tune.	No.
7.7.7.7	Mercy	274	8.8, 8.6.	"Agnus Dei"	333
	Nuremberg	275		Woodworth	334
	Prayer	276		Wyedale	335
	Putney	277	8.8, 8.8, 8.8, 8.8.	Arabia	336
	Redhead	278		Sion	337
	Seymour	279	8.6, 8.8. (Double)	Madison	338
7.7, 7.7, 7.7	Ajalon	280		St. David's	339
	Celano	281	9.8, 9.8.	Cheddon	340
	Crowland	282		Gotha	341
	Dix	283	10.4, 10.4, 10, 10	Lux Benigna	342
	Heathlands	284	10.10, 10.10.	Cecilia	343
	Nassau	285		Ellerton	344
	Sabbath	286		Eventide	345
	Seville	287		Toulon	346
	Temple	288	10.10, 11.11	Beethoven	347
	Wells	289		Hanover	348
7.7, 7.7, 7.7, 7.7	"Hark! the Song"	290		Houghton	349
	Hollingside	291	10.12, 10, 12	Jesmond	350
	Maidstone	292		Kingswood	351
	Mendelssohn	293	11.8, 11.8.	Goderich	352
	St. George	294	11.10, 11.10.	"Come, ye Discon-	
	Thanksgiving	295		solate"	353
	Tichfield	296		Epiphany	354
	Requies	297	11, 11, 11.11	Portuguese Hymn	355
7.7, 8.7, 7,7, 8.7.	Grasmere	298	11, 13, 12, 10.	Nicæa	356
	Protomartyr	299		Trinity	357
	Worship	300	13, 11, 13, 12.	Ems	358
7.7, 8.8, 7.7. (Irreg.).	"Vital Spark"	301			
7.8, 7.8, 7.7	"The Long Home"	302		METRICAL CHANTS.	
8.6, 8.3	"Art thou Weary?"	303			
	Rest	304	L.M. 367	C.M.	372
8.6, 8.6, 6.6, 6.6	Paradise	305	368		373
	Rapture	306	369	8.8.6.	374
8.7, 8.7	Cornell	307	C.M. 370	8.8.4.	375
	Newton Ferns	308	371	Irregular	376
	Vermont	309			
8.7, 8.7, 4.7	Calvary	310		CHANTS AND SENTENCES.	
	Christmas	311			
	Helmsley	312	Te Deum Laudamus	Ousley	359
	Regent's Square	313	" "	Battishill	360
	St. Thomas	314	" "	Robinson	361
	St. Raphael	315	Gloria in Excelsis		362
	Triumph	316	Psalm lxvii.	From Spohr	363
8.7, 8.7, 6.6, 6.7	Worms	317	" "	Mornington	364
8.7, 8.7, 7.7	Evensong	318	Baptismal	Tallis	365
	Gounod	319	The Strain Upraise	Troyte	366
	Zurich	320	Metrical Chant	Elvey	367
8.7, 8.7, 8.7, 8.7	Austria	321	" "	Anon	368
	Benediction	322	" "	Shaw	369
	Granta	323	" "	Robinson	370
	Mant	324	" "	Hopkins	371
	Salvator	325	" "	Sir G. Elvey	372
	Toronto	326	" "	Shaw	373
	Tribute	327	" "	Dixon	374
8.7, 8.7, 8.8.7	Luther's Hymn	328	" "	Troyte	375
8.8.7, 8.8.7	Bonar	329	" "	Downes	376
8.8, 7.7	"Living Water"	330	Sanctus I.	Camidge	377
8.8, 8 4.	Elm Street	331	Sanctus II.	Ebdon	378
	Southport	332	Trisagion and Tersanctus	Anon	379

INDEX II.—ALPHABETICAL.

	No.
Abridge	64
Acclamation	193
Admah	394
Adoration	166
Agnus Dei	333
Ajalon	280
Albion	1
Amsterdam	253
Andrews	65
Angels' Song	2
Antioch	385
Arabia	336
Ariel	204
Arlington	386
Armageddon	162
Arnold	66
Art thou Weary ?	303
Ascension	262
Ashford	263
Asbley	67
Asylum	248
Aubery	68
Aurelia	241
Austria	321
Balerma	69
Bankfield	133
Bartholdy	3
Bath	239
Bedford	70
Bethel	134
Beethoven	347
Belmont	71
Benediction	322
Bethany	218
Bethlehem	128
Bevan	194
Bonar	329
Bonar (C.M.D.)	129
Boylston	135
Bradford	187
Bremen	167
Brighton	108
Bristol	72
Brunswick Chapel	188
Caddo	73
Calcutta	169
Caledon	195
Calvary	310
Cambridge	136
Cana	137
Canada	223
Carlisle	138
Carmel	4
Castleton	170
Cecilia	343

	No.
Celano	281
Celestis Urbs	171
Centennial	189
Cheddon	340
Childhood	74
Christmas	311
Christ Chapel	264
Christ Church	139
Church Triumphant	5
Claremont	75
Clarion	265
Cleansing	404
Cleansing Fountain	400
Colmar	172
Come, ye Disconsolate	353
Come, ye Sinners	401
Comfort	260
Communion	6
Cornell	307
Coronation	387
Coronation (New)	76
Cowley	249
Crasselius	7
Creation	173
Crucifixion	8
Crusader's Hymn	234
Crowland	282
Darwell	196
Dennis	140
Derbe	216
Diademeta	163
Dix	283
Dublin	77
Duke Street	10
Dundee	78
Dresden	9
Eagley	79
Easter Hymn	266
Eaton	174
Eccles	231
Eden	11
Ellacombe	130
Ellarton	344
Elm Street	331
Emmanuel	80
Ems	358
Epiphany	354
Erfurt	12
Ernan	13
Essex	267
Eucharist	14
Euphony	175
Evan	81
Evening Hymn	15
Evensong	318

	No.
Eventide	345
Even Me	402
Ewing	242
Faith	259
Falcon Street	141
Falkirk	254
Farrant	82
Federal Street	16
Fiducia	228
Franconia	142
Fulham	17
Galt	251
Fulneck	232
German Hymn	268
Germany	18
Giessen	176
Gilead	255
Goderich	352
God Save the Queen	224
Going Home	403
Gotha	341
Gounod	819
Granta	323
Grassmere	298
Hamburg	19
Hanover	348
Hark ! the Song	290
Harrington	83
Harrow	269
Hartley	84
Harvington	237
Harwich	215
Harwood	205
Hatfield (C.M.)	85
Haydn	131
Heathlands	284
Hebron	380
Helmsley	312
Hilary	235
Holy Cross	86
Holy Trinity	87
Hollingside	291
Holley	270
Horsley	88
Houghton	349
Howard	89
Huddersfield	90
Hungerford	213
Hursley	20
Innocents	271
Inspruck	206
Intercession	21
Iona	207
Irish	91
Italian Hymn	225

	No.		No.		No.
I am Trusting, Lord, in Thee	405	Munich	29	Saviour, Like a Shepherd	410
I Need Thee Every Hour	406	Nassau	285	Serenity	150
Jazer	92	Nearer Home	165	Sessions	43
Jerusalem	236	Newcastle	30	Seville	287
Jesmond	350	Newhaven	226	Seymour	279
Josiah	256	Newmarket	31	Sheba	230
Jubilee	197	Newton	100	Sherbrook	217
Judah	272	Newton Ferns	308	Shirland	151
Kensington	93	Nicæa	356	Siloam	392
Kingswood	351	Norwood	32	Sion	337
Lancashire	243	Nuremburg	275	Southampton	201
Lanesboro'	94	Old Hundred	33	Southport	332
Leeds	143	Old Saxony	34	Southwell	110
Lennox	396	Olives' Brow	35	Spohr	109
Leomister	164	Olivet	227	St. Agnes	111
Leoni	238	Onward	221	St. Alban	46
Living Water	330	One More Day's Work	407	St. Ann's	112
Lomas	229	Ortonville	390	St. Antolius	258
Love	219	Ossett	36	St. Bernard	113
Lowly and Solemn be	222	Overburg	37	St. Bride	153
Lucca	240	Page	38	St. Catherine	182
Lucerne	190	Paradise	305	St. Crispin	47
Luther's Hymn	328	Pembroke	211	St. Cross	48
Luton	22	Penrhyn	199	St. David	114
Lux Benigna	342	Pentecost	39	St. David's	339
Lydia	388	Peregrinus	101	St. Fulbert	115
Maccabeus	177	Peterborough	102	St. George (L.M.)	49
Madison	338	Portuguese Hymn	355	St. George	294
Madrid	395	Potsdam	145	St. Giles	154
Magdalen College	208	Prague	146	St. Helena	155
Maidstone	292	Prayer	276	St. Hilary	252
Mainzer	23	Prescott	103	St. Martin's	391
Manchester	95	Protomartyr	299	St. Mary Redcliffe	156
Mant	324	Purleigh	212	St. Mary's	116
Mariner's	273	Putney	277	St. Matthias	133
Martyn	398	Rapture	306	St. Michael	157
Martyrdom	96	Redhead	278	St. Olaves	50
Mandesley Street	209	Regent's Square	313	St. Peter	117
Mear	389	Rephidim	104	St. Philip	261
Meditation	409	Requies	297	St. Paul	184
Melbourne	24	Rest	304	St. Raphael	315
Melcombe	25	Rhodes	147	St. Sepulchre	51
Melita	178	Robins	105	St. Serf	63
Mendelssohn	293	Rockingham	40	St. Stephen	118
Mercy	274	Rosehill	106	St. Swithin	203
Meribah	210	Rose Lane	107	St. Theodulph	247
Messiah	97	Rotherfield	41	St Thomas	314
Middlesex	179	Reuben	393	St. Ursula	132
Migdol	381	Russell Place	257	St. Vincent	52
Miles' Lane	98	Russia	382	St. Werburgh	185
Millenium	198	Rutherford	246	Steggall	202
Milton	26	Sabbath (L.M.)	42	Stella	180
Mirfield	99	Sabbath (S.M.)	148	Stour Valley	214
Missionary	244	Sabbath	286	Stratham	44
Monmouth	191	Safe in the Arms of Jesus	408	Sullivan	220
Montgomery	27	Salisbury	108	Sunset	62
Morning Hymn	28	Salvator	325	Supplication	152
Morning Light	245	Samuel	200	Susannah	45
Mount Ephraim	144	Sarah	149	Swaffham	181

	No.		No.		No.
Tallis' Ordinal	119	Trinity	357	Wavertree	58
Temple	288	Triumph	316	Wells	289
Thanksgiving	295	Truro	54	What a Friend we have	416
Thatcher	158	Tuam	159	Whitby	125
The Child's Desire	411	Twilight	259	Whitefield	161
The Long Home	302	Unity	413	Wilt Thou Hear the Voice	415
The Pilgrim's Mission	414	Uxbridge	383	Windham	59
The Precious Name	412	Valete	186	Woodworth	334
Thornton	233	Vermont	309	Worcester	60
Tichfield	296	Vespers	55	Work, for the Night is	417
Toplady	397	Vital Spark	301	Worms	317
Toronto	326	Walsal	123	Worship	300
Tottenham	120	Ward	56	Wyedale	335
Toulon	346	Wareham	61	York	126
Trenton	121	Warksworth	160	Zephyr	384
Tribute	327	Warrington	57	Zurich (6.8's)	192
Turin	53	Warwick	124	Zurich	320
Trinity (C.M.)	122	Watchman	399	Zwingle	127

INDEX III.—HYMNS.

NOTE.—The first verse of the following Hymns are used in this work to accompany the Music, by way of illustration ; but a suitable Tune to *any hymn* may be found by reference to the Metrical Index.

No. of Hymn.	No. of Tune.	No. of Hymn.	No. of Tune.	No. of Hymn.	No. of Tune.	No. of Hymn.	No. of Tune.
1	71, 373	119	202	201	307	344	88
9	61, 369	122	200, 196	204	260, 261	346	65, 388
10	27	123	234	205	330	347	67, 108
12	147, 322	124	235, 236	206	43	349	347
13	148	125	231	210	401	351	350, 351
14	141	126	241	211	197	352	409
15	146, 393	127	7	213	303	353	214
16	170	134	115	214	353	355	336
17	179	135	77	217	269	360	86
20	185	136	70	218	297	361	129
24	356, 357	137	117	220	101	362	93
25	226	141	132	222	289	366	26
27	225	139	120	225	308	369	6
28	315	142	293	233	135	374	166
29	349	144	323	234	137	375	248
31	324	145	311	239	118	381	175
35	212	146	354	242	400	384	47, 368
37	209	147	54	243	405, 292	389	389
39	238	148	41	245	277	392	90
39	237	140	250	246	153	394	113
41	94	150	251	247	152, 160	396	119
43	68	152	8, 14	248	145	397	72
45	127	157	151	253	332	398	219
46	83	160	280, 397	254	335	399	218, 220
50	33	161	270	255	333, 334, 374	400	227
61	188	162	215	256	402	403	155
62	189	164	329	258	382	409	276
64	18	165	123	261	29	413	257
67	2	168	309	262	30	415	252
69	232	169	327	264	168	419	50, 380
70	352	747	126	267	182	420	22
75	395	172	16	270	285	421	49
80	51	174	266	273	288	423	187
83	40	175	313	274	287	427	111
88	87	176	267	275	283	434	320
92	110	177	262, 275	280	95	435	255
93	122	178	194	284	384	436	326
97	342	183	69	288	210	438	414
98	180	184	391	290	211	444	91
99	173	186	92	297	167	445	64
104	63	190	172	300	109	450	206
105	37	192	381	301	112	452	45
108	98, 387	193	13	305	53	454	163
111	76, 385	194	4	308	82, 116	462	150
112	75	195	282	309	106	467	60
113	99	196	274	314	339	468	23
115	204	197	279	317	254	470	79
117	291, 398	198	138	337	161	472	386
118	296	199	233	331	253	473	298, 299

No. of Hymn.	No. of Tune.	No. of Hymn.	No. of Tune.	No. of Hymn.	No. of Tune.	No. of Hymn.	No. of Tune.
474	300	616	164	738	399	837	415
476	325	622	305, 306	740	265	838	411
479	355	628	337	741	290	846	34
484	19	630	217	743	245	847	44
485	35	632	376	744	244	850	59
486	176	636	370	746	221	851	3
488	174, 177	642	21	747	126	852	48
492	78	643	55	750	114	854	149
493	104	645	42	753	143	857	301
496	142	646	286	754	136	858	302
500	331, 375	647	199	756	157	861	239, 240
501	228, 230	648	124	758	140	862	222
502	272	652	133	760	413	864	338
503	278	655	268	762	58	865	358
504	249	656	344	763	403	877	310
506	317	657	196	764	62	879	312
512	205	659	191	770	264	880	193, 198
516	107	661	189	773	416	881	328
519	81	662	134	774	412	882	281
520	96	664	321	775	304	885	56
525	404	666	316	776	246	889	9
526	158	669	12	779	229	891	201
528	156	671	121	780	407	892	216
531	52	672	10	781	406	902	1, 85
543	256	674	38	782	417	903	223
549	184	675	271	783	343	904	224
550	171	676	203	784	345, 346	908	243
558	17	684	144	786	348	910	294
559	66, 371	690	73	801	213	917	154
560	24	701	89	804	20	921	159
561	390	702	102	805	32	922	314
568	97	705	340, 341	806	46	923	103
580	190	706	57	807	28	925	84, 372
581	192	708	30	808	15	928	367
584	208	709	383	809	11	933	178
586	207	710	31	812	258, 259		
591	295	712	36	815	100		
594	263	718	5	818	74	Chant 15	359
602	130	721	247	819	392	Doxology 19	362
607	131	728	105	824	273	" 18	363
608	80	730	169	825	318, 319	Chant 16	365
609	128	731	181	826	284	Doxology 17	366
613	186, 394	736	162	829	408	Sanctus	377, 378
615	165	737	195	834	410	Trisagion	379

METHODIST TUNE BOOK.

1.

B. Livins.

Cheerful. O King of kings, thy bles - sing shed On our an -

- oint - ed Sovereign's head! And, look - ing from thy ho - ly

heav'n, Pro - tect the crown thy - self hast giv'n.

[1]

2.

Hymn 67.—Angels' Song.—L. M.

Orlando Gibbons.

Moderate.

E - ter - nal depth of love di - vine, In Je - sus, God with us, display'd;

How bright thy beaming glor - ies shine! How wide thy heal - ing streams are spread!

Hymn 851.—Bartholdy.—L. M.

Mendelssohn.

Slowly. Unveil thy bosom, faith - ful tomb; Take this new trea - sure to thy trust,

And give these sac - red rel - ics room To slumber in the si - lent dust.

[2]

4.   Hymn 194.—Carmel.—L M.   *Wallhead.*

Moderate. Come, Holy Spirit, raise our songs, To reach the wonders of the day,

When with thy fie - ry clov - en tongues Thou didst those glorious scenes dis - play.

5.   Hymn 718.—Church Triumphant.—L. M.   *J. W. Elliot.*

Cheerful. O Christ, the Lord of heav'n, to thee, Cloth'd with all ma - jes - ty divine,

E - ter - nal pow'r and glo - ry be, E - ter - nal praise of right is thine!

[3]

6. **Hymn 369.—Communion.—L. M.** *Dr. Miller.*

Moderate. God of my life, through all my days, My grateful powers shall sound thy praise;

My song shall wake with open - ing light, And cheer the dark and sil - ent night.

7. **Hymn 127.—Crasselius.—L. M.** *Crasselius.*

Cheerful. Je - sus, thou Joy of lov - ing hearts! Thou Fount of life! thou Light of men!

From the best bliss that earth im - parts, We turn un - filled to thee a - gain.

[4]

8. **Hymn 152.—Crucifixion.—L. M.**

Slow. When I sur-vey the wondrous cross, On which the Prince of glo-ry died,

My richest gain I count but loss, And pour con-tempt on all my pride.

9. **Hymn 889.—Dresden.—L. M.** *From Mozart.*

Moderate. E-ter-nal Source of ev-'ry joy, Well may thy praise our lips em-ploy,

While in thy tem-ple we ap-pear, Whose goodness crowns the circling year.

[5]

10. Hymn 672.—**Duke Street.**—L. M.   *John Hatton.*

Cheerful. O Lord of hosts, whose glor - y fills The bounds of the e - ter - nal hills,

And yet vouchsafes, in Chris - tian lands, To dwell in tem - ples made with hands.

---

11. Hymn 809.—**Eden.**—L. M.   *Dr. L. Mason.*

Moderate. My God, how end - less is thy love! Thy gifts are ever - y even - ing new;

And morn - ing mercies from a - bove, Gently dis - til like ear - ly dew.

[6]

12.　　　　　**Hymn 669.—Erfurt.—L. M.**　　　*Luther.*

Bold. This stone to thee in faith we lay To thee this tem - ple, Lord, we build:

Thy power and good - ness here dis - play, And be it with thy presence filled.

13.　　　　　**Hymn 193.—Ernan.—L. M.**　　　*Dr. L. Mason.*

Cheerful. O Spirit of the liv - ing God, In all thy plen - i - tude of grace.

Where'er the foot of man hath trod, Descend on our a - pos - tate race.

[7]

14.

Hymn 152.—Eucharist.—L. M.

J. B. Woodbury.

Slowly. When I survey the wond - rous cross On which the Prince of glor - y died,

My richest gain I count but loss, And pour con - tempt on all my pride

15.

Hymn 808.—Evening Hymn.—L. M.

Thomas Tallis.

Moderate. Glor - y to thee, my God, this night, For all the bless - ings of the light:

Keep me, O keep me, King of kings, Be - neath thine own al - might - y wings!

[8]

16. Hymn 172.—*Federal Street.*—L. M.   *H. K. Oliver.*

Slowly. He dies! the Friend of sin-ners dies! Lo! Salem's daughters weep around!

A solemn dark-ness veils the skies, A sudden trembling shakes the ground.

17. Hymn 558.—*Fulham.*—L. M.   *W. Harrison.*

Moderate. Holy, and true, and righte-ous Lord, I wait to prove thy per-fect will,

Be mindful of thy gracious word, And stamp me with thy Spir-its seal.

[9]

18.   Hymn 64.—Germany.—L. M.   *Beethoven.*

Moderate. Unchangea - ble, all - per - fect Lord, Es - sen - tial life's un - bound - ed sea,

What lives and moves, lives by thy word; It lives, and moves, and is from thee.

19.   Hymn 484.—Hamburg.—L. M.   *Dr. L. Mason.*

Slowly. O thou, to whose all - search - ing sight The darkness shin - eth as the light,

Search, prove my heart; it pants for thee; O burst these bonds, and set it free!

[10]

20.   **Hymn 804.—Kursley.—L. M.**   *Huguenot Melody*

Moderate. Sun of my soul, thou Saviour dear, It is not night if thou be near;

Oh, may no earth-born cloud a - rise To hide thee from thy ser - vant's eyes.

---

21.   **Hymn 642.—Intercession.—L. M.**   *Rev. Dr. Dykes.*

Moderate. Lord of the Sab - bath, hear our vows, On this thy day, in this thy house;

And own, as grateful sac - ri - fice, The songs which from thy ser - vants rise.

[11]

22.

Hymn 420.—Luton.—L. M.

Rev. G. Burder.

Cheerful. My gracious Lord, I own thy right To ever-y ser-vice I can pay,

And call it my su-preme de-light To hear thy dic-tates, and o-bey.

23.

Hymn 468.—Mainzer.—L. M.

Dr. Mainzer.

Slowly. God is the re-fuge of his saints, When storms of sharp dis-tress in-vade;

Ere we can off-er our complaints, Be-hold him pre-sent with his aid.

[12]

24. Hymn 560.—Melbourne.—L. M. *Dr. Ford.*

Slowly. O God, most merci - ful and true, Thy na - ture to my soul impart: Stablish with me the

covenant new, And write perfec - tion on my heart, And write per - fection on my heart.

25. Hymn 927.—Welcombe.—L. M. *S. Webbe.*

Moderate. O thou who hast, in ever - y age, Thy trust - ing peo - ple safe - ly led,

On us, who in thy work en - gage, Thy Spir - it's guid - ing in - fluence shed.

[13]

26.

W. H. Gladstone.

Moderate. In - to thy gracious hands I fall, And with the arms of faith em - brace;

O King of Glor - y, hear my call, O raise me, heal me, by thy grace!

27.

Hymn 10.—Montgomery.—L. M.

Stanley.

Cheerful. Fa - ther, whose ev - er - last - ing love Thy on - ly son for sin - ners gave;

Whose grace to all did free - ly move, And sent him down the world to save.

28. Hymn 807. — *Morning Hymn.* — L M.   *F. H. Barthelemon.*

Cheerful. A - wake, my soul, and with the sun Thy dai - ly stage of du - ty run,

Shake off dull sloth, and joy - ful rise To pay thy morn - ing sac - ri - fice.

29. Hymn 261. — *Munich.* — L M.   *German.*

Slow. O thou that hear'st when sin - ners cry, Tho all my crimes be - fore thee lie,

Be - hold me not with an - gry look, But blot their memory from thy book.

[15]

30.

Hymn 708.—Newcastle.—L. M.

T. Shoel.

Bold. The Lord is King, and earth sub-mits, Howe'er im-pa-tient,

to his sway; Be-tween the Cher-u-bim he sits, And makes his

restless foes o-bey, And makes his rest-less foes o-bey.

31.

Hymn 710.—Newmarket.—L. M.

Dr. Wainwright.

Cheerful. Let Zi-on in her King re-joice, Tho' Satan rage, and kingdoms rise;

He ut - ters his al - might - y voice, The nations melt, the tu - mult dies.

32.   Hymn 805.—Norwood.—L. M.   *W. H. Hart.*

Moderate. How do thy mer - cies close me round! For - ev - er

be thy name a - dored; I blush in all things

to a - bound; The ser - vant is a - bove his Lord.

B   [17]

33.

Hymn 50.—Old Hundred.—L. M.

G. Franc, 1543.

Bold. All peo - ple that on earth do dwell, Sing to the Lord with cheerful voice:

Him serve with fear, his praise forth tell, Come ye be - fore him, and re - joice.

34.

Hymn 846.—Old Saxony.—L. M.

German.

Slow. Al - migh - ty mak - er of my frame, Teach me the measure of my days,

Teach me to know how frail I am, And spend the rem - nant to thy praise.

[18]

39.

Hymn 262.—Pentecost.—L. M.

William Boyd

Slowly. With broken heart and contrite sigh, A trembling sin - ner, Lord, I cry;

Thy pardoning grace is rich and free; O God, be mer - ci - ful to me

38.

Hymn 114.—Ussell.—L. M.

Widdop.

Lively. E - ter - nal Fa - ther, thou hast said, That Christ all glor - y shall ob - tain;

That he who once a sufferer bled Shall o'er the world a conqueror reign.

[19]

33.

Hymn 50.—Old Hundred.—L. M

G. Franc, 1543.

Bold. All peo - ple that on earth do dwell, Sing to the Lord with cheerful voice:

Him serve with fear, his praise forth tell, Come ye be - fore him, and re - joice.

38.

Hymn 674.—Page.—L. M.

G. M. Garrett.

Moderate. Great God, thy watchful care we bless, Which guards these sacred courts in peace;

Nor dare tu - multuous foes in - vade, To fill thy wor - ship - pers with dread.

[20]

39.

Hymn 262.—Pentecost.—L. M.

William Boyd

Slowly. With broken heart and contrite sigh, A trembling sin - ner, Lord, I cry;

Thy pardoning grace is rich and free; O God, be mer - ci - ful to me

---

40.

Hymn 83.—Rockingham.—L. M.

Dr. L. Mason.

Slowly. O thou, whom all thy saints a - dore, We now with all thy saints a - gree,

And bow our in - most souls be - fore Thy glorious, aw - ful Ma - jes - ty.

[21]

41.

Hymn 148.—Rotherfield.—L. M.

A. H. Browne.

Cheerful. To us a Child of roy-al birth, Heir of the pro-mis-es, is given;

Th' In-vis-i-ble ap-pears on earth, The Son of man, the God of heaven.

42.

Hymn 645—Sabbath.—L. M.

H. P. Smith.

Moderate. Sweet is the sunlight af-ter rain, And sweet the sleep which fol-lows pain

And sweet-ly steals the Sabbath rest Up-on the world's work-wearied breast.

[22]

43. **Hymn 206.—Sessions.—L. M.** *L. O. Emmers.—*

Slowly. Come, sinners, to the gospel feast; Let ev - 'ry soul be Jesus' guest;

Ye need not *one* be left behind, For God hath bid - den *all* mankind.

44. **Hymn 847.—Stratham.—L. M.** *Stratham.*

Cheerful. I know that my Re - deem - er lives, He lives, and on the earth shall stand;

And though to worms my flesh he gives, My dust lies numbered in his hands.

45. Hymn 452.—Susannah.—L. M. *Dr. S. S. Wesley.*

Moderate. Je - sus, my Saviour, Brother, Friend, On whom I cast my ev - 'ry care,

On whom for all things I de - pend; In - spire, and then ac - cept, my prayer.

46. Hymn 806.—St. Alban.—L. M. *St. Alban's Tune Book.*

Moderate. New eve - ry morning is the love Our wakening and up - ris - ing prove:

Through sleep and darkness safe - ly brought, Restored to life, and power, and thought.

[24]

47. Hymn 384.—St. Crispin.—L. M. *Sir G. J. Elvey.*

Slowly. From eve - ry stormy wind that blows, From eve - ry swelling tide of woes,

There is a calm, a sure re - treat; Tis found beneath the mer - cy - seat.

48. Hymn 852.—St. Cross.—L. M. *Rev. Dr Dykes.*

Slow Asleep in Jes - us! bless - ed sleep, From which none ev - er wakes to weep!

pp

A calm and un - disturb'd re - pose, Un - broken by the last of foes.

pp

49. Hymn 421.—St. George.—L. M. *R. Harrison.*

Cheerful. Go, la - bour on; spend and be spent, Thy joy to
do the Fa - ther's will; It is the way the
Mas - ter went; Should not the ser - vant tread it still?

50. Hymn 419.—St. Olaves.—L. M. *Hudson.*

Lively. Forth in thy name, O Lord, I go, My dai - ly

[26]

St. Olaves.—*Continued.*

la - bour   to   pur - sue,   Thee,   on - ly   thee   re-

solv'd   to   know,   In   all   I   think,   or   speak,   or   do.

51.   Hymn 80.—St. Sepulchre.—L. M.   *George Cooper*

Cheerful. How pleasant, how di - vine - ly fair, O Lord of hosts, thy dwellings are

With strong de - sire my spir - it faints To meet th' as - sem - blies of thy saints.

[27]

52.

Hymn 531.—St. Vincent.—L. M.   *Adapted by C. E. Willing.*

Moderate. Come, Saviour, Jesus, from a - bove! As - sist me with thy heavenly grace;

Emp - ty my heart of earth - ly love, And for thy - self pre - pare the place.

53.

Hymn 305.—Turin.—L. M.   *Picraccini.*

Moderate. Why should I till to - morrow stay For what thou wouldst be - stow to - day;

What thou more will - ing art to give Than I to ask, or to re - ceive?

[28]

54.

Hymn 147.—Truro.—L. M.

Dr. Burney

Bold. Sing, all in heav'n, at Je-su's birth, Glo-ry to God, and peace on earth·

In-car-nate love in Christ is seen, Pure mer-cy and good-will to men.

55.

Hymn 643.—Vespers.—L. M.

J. W. Elliot.

Moderate. Sweet is the work, my God, my King, To praise thy name, give thanks, and sing;

To show thy love by morn-ing light, And talk of all thy truth at night.

[29]

Hymn 885.—Ward.—L. M.

Dr. L. Mason.

Slow. The day of wrath, that dreadful day, When heav'n and earth shall pass a - way!

What pow'r shall be the sin - ner's stay? How shall he meet that dread - ful day!

57.

Hymn 706.—Warrington.—L. M.

Rev. Ralph Harrison.

Great God, whose u - ni - ver - sal sway The known and unknown worlds o - bey,

Cheerful.

Now give the kingdom to thy Son, Ex - tend his power, ex - alt his throne

58. Hymn 762.—Wavertree.—L. M. W Shore.

Moderate. My soul, thro' my Re - deem - er's care, Saved from the sec - ond death I feel,

My eyes from tears of dark des - pair, My feet from fall - ing in - to hell.

---

59. Hymn 850.—Windham.—L. M. D. Read

Slow. Shrinking from the cold hand of death, I soon shall ga - ther up my feet;

Shall soon re - sign this fleet - ing breath, And die, my fathers' God to meet.

[31]

60. **Hymn 467.—Worcester.—L. M.**

Cheerful. Arm of the Lord, a - wake! a - wake! Thine own im - mor - tal strength put on!

With terror clothed, hell's kingdom shake, And cast thy foes with fu - ry down!

61. **Hymn 9.—Wareham.—L. M.** *Knapp*

Bold. From all that dwell be - low the skies Let the Cre - a - tor's praise a - rise:

Let the Re - deemer's name be sung, Thro' eve - ry land, by eve - ry tongue.

62. Hymn 764.—Sunset.—L. M. (Double). *Martin Luta.*

Moderate. At ev - en, ere the sun was set, The sick, O Lord, a - round thee lay;

O in what di - vers pains they met! O with what joy they went a - way!

Once more 'tis ev - en - tide, and we Oppress'd with various ills draw near;

What if thy form we can - not see, We know and feel that thou art here.

[33]

Moderate. The spacious fir - ma - ment on high, With all the blue e - thereal sky,

And spangled heavens, a shi - ning frame, Their great O - ri - gi - nal proclaim.

Th' un - wearied sun, from day to day, Does his Cre - a - tor's power dis - play.

And pub - lish - es to eve - ry land The work of an al - migh - ty hand.

END OF LONG METRE TUNES

64.   Hymn 445.—Abridge.—C. M.   *Isaac Smith.*

Cheerful. Thou, Lord, hast blest my go - ing out, O bless my com - ing in!

Com pass my weakness round a - bout, And keep me safe from sin.

65.   Hymn 346.—Andrews.—C. M.   *Rev. John Black.*

Moderate. Come — let us who in Christ believe, Our common Sa - viour praise:

To him with joy - ful voi - ces give The glo - ry of his grace.

[35]

66.

Hymn 559.—Arnold.—C. M.

Dr. S. Arnold.

Moderate. For ev - er here my rest shall be, Close to thy bleed - ing side;

This all my hope, and all my plea, For me the Saviour died!

67.

Hymn 347.—Ashley.—C. M.

Rev. M. Madan.

Cheerful. Sal - vation! O the joy - ful sound! What plea - sure to our ears!

A sovereign balm to ev' - ry wound, A cord - ial for our fears.

Ashley.—*Continued.*

CHORUS. Glo - ry, honour, praise, and pow - er, Be un - to the Lamb for ev - er

Jesus Christ is our Redeemer. Hallelujah, Hallelujah. Hallelujah. praise the Lord.

---

68. **Hymn 43.—Aubery.—C. M.** *Vincent.*

Cheerful. Thy cease - less un - ex - haust - ed love, Un - mer - it - ed and free,

De - lights our e - vil to remove, And help our mis - e - ry.

[37]

69.

Hymn 183.—Balerma.—C M. *Adapted by R. Simpson.*

Moderate. Spi - rit di - vine, at - tend our prayers, And make this house thy home,

Descend with all thy gracious powers, O come, great Spi - rit, come!

70.

Hymn 136.—Bedford.—C. M. *W. Wheall.*

Slowly. With joy we me - di - tate the grace Of our High Priest a - bove:

His heart is made of ten - der - ness, And yearns with pity - ing love.

[38]

'71.   Hymn 1.—Belmont.—C. M.   *Webb.*

Cheerful. O for a thousand tongues to sing My great Re - deem - er's praise,

The glo - ries of my God and King, The triumphs of his grace!

72.   Hymn 397.—Bristol.—C. M.   *Dr. Hodges.*

Moderate. Prayer is the soul's sin - cere de - sire, Ut - tered or un - ex - pressed,

The mo - tion of a hid - den fire, That trembles in the breast.

73. Hymn 690.—Caddo.—C. M. *W. B. Bradbury.*

Moderate. O Lord, while we con - fess the worth Of this the out - ward seal,

Do thou the truths here - in set forth To ev' - ry heart re - veal.

74. Hymn 818.—Childhood.—C. M. *Rev. C. J. Dickinson.*

Cheerful. Come, Christian chil - dren, come, and raise Your voice with one ac - cord;

Come sing in joy - ful songs of praise The glo - ries of your Lord.

[40]

75.   Hymn 112.—Claremont.—C. M.   *J. Foster.*

Cheerful. How sweet the name of Jes - us sounds In a be - liev - er's ear!

It soothes his sorrows, heals his wounds, And drives a - way his fear.

76.   Hymn 111.—Coronation (New).—C. M.   *Rev. Dr. Dykes.*

Cheerful. Joy to the world! the Lord is come; Let earth re - ceive her King;

Let ev' - ry heart pre - pare him room, And heaven and na - ture sing.

[41]

77.   **Hymn 135.—Dublin.—C. M.**   *Sir J. Stevenson.*

Thou great Re - deem - er, dy - ing Lamb, We love to hear of thee;
Moderate.

No mus - ic's like thy charm - ing name, Nor half so sweet can be.

78.   **Hymn 492.—Dundee.—C. M.**   *Scotch Psalter, 1615.*

Moderate. Out of the depths to thee I cry, Whose faint - ing foot - steps trod

The paths of our hu - man - i - ty, In - car - nate Son of God!

79. Hymn 470.—Eagley.—C. M. *J. Walch.*

Moderate. O for a faith that will not shrink, Tho' pressed by ev' - ry foe,

That will not trem - ble on the brink Of a - ny earth - ly woe!

80. Hymn 608.—Emmanuel.—C. M. *Beethoven.*

Lively. On Jor - dan's stor - my banks I stand, And cast a wish - ful eye

To Canaan's fair and hap - py land, Where my pos - ses - sions lie.

[43]

81. Hymn 519.—Evan.—C. M. *Rev. W. H. Havergall.*

Cheerful. Jes - us hath died that I might live, Might live to God a lone;

In him e - ter - nal life re - ceive, And be in spi - rit one.

82. Hymn 308.—Farrant.—C. M. *R. Farrant, 1585.*

Slowly. God is in this and ev' - ry place; But, O, how dark and void

To me!—'tis one great wil - der - ness, This earth with - out my God.

[44]

83. Hymn 46.—**Harrington.**—C. M. *Dr. Harrington.*

Cheerful. Fa - ther of me, and all man - kind, And all the hosts a - bove,

Let ev' - ry un - der - stand - ing mind U - nite to praise thy love.

84. Hymn 925.—**Hartley.**—C. M. *James Turle.*

Moderate. Father su - preme, by whom we live, Thou who art God a - lone,

Our songs of grateful praise re - ceive, And make our hearts thy throne.

[45]

85.

Hymn 909.—Hatfield.—C. M.

Cheerful. Fountain of mer - cy, God of love, How rich thy bounties are!

The roll - ing sea - sons, as they move, Pro - claim thy con - stant care.

86.

Hymn 360.—Holy Cross.—C. M.

Moderate. Talk with us, Lord, thy - self re - veal, While here o'er earth we rove;

Speak to our hearts, and let us feel The kindling of thy love.

87. Hymn 88.—Holy Trinity—C. M.   *J. Barnby.*

Moderate. My God, how won - der - ful thou art, Thy ma - jes - ty how bright,

How beau - ti - ful thy mer - cy - seat In depth of burn - ing light!

88. Hymn 344.—Horsley.—C. M.   *Wm. Horsley.*

Cheerful. Hap - py the heart where gra - ces reign, Where love in - spires the breast;

Love is the brightest of the train, And per - fects all the rest.

89.

Hymn 01.—Howard.—C. M.

Dr. Howard.

Moderate. Ac - cord - ing to thy gra - cious word, In meek hu - mil - i - ty,

This will I do, my dy - ing Lord, I will re - mem - ber thee!

90.

Hymn 92.—Huddersfield.—C. M.

Madan.

Moderate. O Sun of Righteousness, a - rise, With healing in thy wing

To my dis - eas'd, my faint - ing soul. Life and sal - va - tion bring.

91.　　　**Hymn 444.—Irish.—C. M.**　*Arranged from Isaac Smith.*

Moderate. I want a prin - ci - ple with - in Of jeal - ous, god - ly fear,

A sen - si - bil - i - ty - of sin, A pain, to feel it near.

92.　　　**Hymn 186.—Mazer.—C. M.**　*A. E. Tozer.*

Moderate. Sovereign of all the worlds on high, Al - low my hum - ble claim;

Nor, while un - worthy, I draw nigh, Dis - dain a Fa - ther's name.

D　　　　[49]

93. **Hymn 362.—Kensington.—C. M.** *Braine.*

Moderate. My Shepherd will sup - ply my need, JE - HOV - AH is his name;

In pas - tures fresh he makes me feed, Be - side the liv - ing stream.

94. **Hymn 41.—Lanesboro'.—C. M.**

Cheerful. Come, Let us join our cheerful songs With angels round the throne; Ten thousand thousand

are their tongues, Ten thousand thousand are their tongues, But all their joys are one.

95.   Hymn 280.—*Manchester.*—C. M.   *Dr. R. Wainwright.*

Slowly. O for a clos-er walk with God, A calm and heaven-ly frame;

A light to shine up-on the road That leads me to the Lamb!

96.   Hymn 520.—*Martyrdom.*—C. M.   *Hugh Wilson.*

Moderate. What is our call-ing's glorious hope, But inward ho-li-ness!

For this to Jes-us I look up, I calm-ly wait for this.

[51]

97.   Hymn 568.—**Messiah.**—C. M.   *Handel.*

Slowly I know that my Re - deem - er lives, And ev - er prays for me;

A to - ken of his love he gives, A pledge of lib - er - ty.

98.   Hymn 108.—**Miles' Lane.**—C. M.   *Shrubsole.*

Cheerful. All hail the pow'r of Jes - us' name, Let an - gels prostrate fall; Bring forth the royal

di - a - dem, And crown him, crown him, crown him, crown him Lord of all.

[52]

99.　　　　Hymn 113.—**Mirfield.**—C. M.　　　*A. Cottman.*

Cheerful. Plung'd in a gulf of dark de - spair We wretch - ed sin - ners lay,

With - out one cheer - ful beam of hope, Or spark of glimm'ring day.

100.　　　　Hymn 815.—**Newton.**—C. M.　　　*Jackson.*

Moderate. Hap - py the home when God is there, And love fills ev' - ry breast;

When one their wish, and one their prayer, And one their heavenly rest.

[53]

101. Hymn 220.—Peregrinus.—C. M. *A. R. Gaul.*

Moderate. Re - turn, O wand'rer, to thy home, Thy Fa - ther calls for thee;

No longer now an exile roam In guilt and mis - e - ry. Re - turn! Re - turn!

---

102. Hymn 702.—Peterborough.—C. M. *Rev. Ralph Harrison.*

Moderate. In mem'ry of the Saviour's love, We keep the sa - cred feast,

Where ev' - ry humble, contrite heart, Is made a wel - come guest.

103. Hymn 923.—Prescott.—C. M.

Slowly. She lov'd her Sa - viour, and to him Her costliest pre - sent brought:

To crown his head, or grace his name, No gift too rare she thought.

---

104. Hymn 493.—Rephidim.—C M

Moderate. O thou who driest the mourner's tear, How dark this world would be,

If when de - ceiv'd and wounded here, We could not fly to thee!

[55]

105.   **Hymn 728.—Robbins.—C. M.**   *C. Draper.*

Bold. Jes - us, im - mor - tal King, a - rise; As - sert thy right - ful sway,

Till earth, sub - dued, its trib - ute brings, And dis - tant lands o - bey.

106.   **Hymn 309.—Rose Hill.—C. M.**   *Dr. Ford.*

Moderate. With glorious clouds en - compass'd round, Whom an - gels dim - ly see,

Will the Un - search - a - ble be found, Or God ap - pear to me?

[56]

Rose Hill.—*Continued.*

Will the Un - search - a - ble be found, Or God ap - pear to me?

107. Hymn 516.—Rose Lane.—C. M.   *T. Clark.*

Moderate. Jes - us, to thee I now can fly, On whom my

help is laid; Oppress'd by sins, I lift my eye, And

see the sha - dows fade, And see the sha - dows fade.

[57]

108. Hymn 347.—**Salisbury.**—C. M. *Ravenscroft and Turvey.*

Cheerful. Sal - va - tion! O the joy - ful sound! What pleasure to our ears!

A sovereign balm to ev' - ry wound, A cor - dial for our fears.

CHORUS.

Lively. Glory, honour, praise, and power, Be un - to the Lamb for ev - er; Jesus Christ is our Redeemer:

Hal - le - lu - jah! Hal - le - lu - jah! Hal - le - lu - jah! praise the Lord!

[58]

109. Hymn 300.—**Spohr.**—C. M.   *Dr. L. Spohr.*

Slowly. As pants the hart for cool - ing streams, When heat - ed in the chase,

So pants my soul, O God, for thee, And thy re - fresh - ing grace.

110. Hymn 92.—**Southwell.**—C. M.   *H. S. Irons.*

Cheerful. When all thy mer - cies, O my God, My ris - ing soul sur - veys,

Transport - ed with the view, I'm lost In won - der, love, and praise.

[59]

111.

Dr. Dykes.

Slowly. Lord, as to thy dear cross we flee, And pray to be for - giv'n,

O let thy life our pat - tern be, And form our souls for heaven.

112.

Hymn 301.—St. Ann's.—C. M.

Dr. Crofts.

Moderate. Come, let us to the Lord our God With con - trite hearts re - turn;

Our God is gracious, nor will leave The des - o - late to mourn.

[60]

113. Hymn 394.—St. Bernard.—C. M. *W. Richardson.*

Moderate. Lord, when we bend be - fore thy throne, And our con - fes - sions pour,

Teach us to feel the sins we own, And hate what we de - plore.

114. Hymn 760.—St. David.—C. M. *Playford's Psalter, 1671.*

Moderate. Be - hold us, Lord, a lit - tle space From dai - ly tasks set free,

And met with - in thy ho - ly place To rest a - while with thee.

[61]

115. Hymn 134.—St. Fulbert.—C. M. *Dr. Gauntlett.*

Moderate. Thou art the Way; to thee a-lone From sin and death we flee

And he who would the Fa-ther seek, Must seek him, Lord, by thee.

116. Hymn 308.—St. Mary's.—C. M. *Dr. John Blow, 1670.*

Slowly. God is in this and ev'-ry place; But, O, how dark and void

To me!—'tis one great wil-der-ness, This earth with-out my God.

[62]

117.   Hymn 137.—St. Peter.—C. M.   *A. R. Reinagle.*

Moderate. The head that once was crown'd with thorns, Is crown'd with glo - ry now;

A roy - al di - a - dem a - dorns The migh - ty Vic - tor's brow.

118.   Hymn 239.—St. Stephen.—C. M.   *Rev. W. Jones.*

Moderate. Jes - us, in thee all fulness dwells, And all for wretched man;

Fill ev' - ry want my spi - rit feels, And break off ev' - ry chain!

[63]

119.

Cheerful. Our Fa - ther, God, who art in heav'n, All hallow'd be thy name;

Thy kingdom come; thy will be done In heav'n and earth the same.

120.

Hymn 139.—Tottenham.—C. M.   *Greatorex.*

Lively. Hark, the glad sound, the Sav - iour comes! The Saviour promis'd long;

Let ev' - ry heart ex - ult with joy, And ev' - ry voice be song!

[64]

121. Hymn 671.—Trenton.—C. M. *J. Barnby.*

Cheerful. O thou, whose own vast tem - ple stands Built o - ver earth and sea,

Ac - cept the walls that human hands Have rais'd to wor - ship thee!

---

122. Hymn 93.—Trinity.—C. M.

Moderate. Let ev' - ry tongue thy good - ness speak, Thou sovereign Lord of all;

Thy strength'ning hands up - hold the weak, And raise the poor that fall.

123.

Hymn 165.—Walsal.—C. M.

H. Purcell, 1685.

Slowly. Be - hold the Sa - viour of man - kind Nail'd to the shame - ful tree! How vast the love that him in - clin'd To bleed and die for thee!

124.

Hymn 648.—Warwick.—C. M.

Samuel Stanley.

Cheerful. Come, let us join with one ac - cord In

[66]

Warwick.—*Continued.*

hymns   a - round   the   throne;   This   is   the

day   our   ri - sing   Lord   Hath   made   and   call'd   his   own.

---

125.   **Hymn 171.—Whitby.—C. M.**   *Stratham.*

Moderate.   Ye   hum - ble souls, that   seek   the Lord,   Chase   all   your fears   a - way;

And   bow   with rap - ture   down   to   see   The   place   where Je - sus   lay.

[67]

126. **Hymn 747.—York.—C. M.** Scotch Psalter, 1615.

Joyful. All praise to our Re - deem - ing Lord Who joins us by his grace,

And bids us, each to each re - stor'd, To - geth - er seek his face.

---

127. **Hymn 45.—Zwingle.—C. M.** *Knecht.*

Cheerful. O God, our strength, to thee our song With grate - ful hearts we raise;

To thee, and thee a - lone, be - long All worship, love, and praise.

128.   Hymn 609.—Bethlehem.—C. M. D.   *Old Melody, arranged by Sir A. Sullivan.*

Lively. There is a land of pure delight, Where saints immortal reign;

In - fi - nite day ex - cludes the night, And pleasures ban - ish pain.

There ev - er - last - ing spring a - bides, And nev - er - withering flowers;

Death, like a nar - row sea, di - vides This heavenly land from ours.

[69]

129. Hymn 361.—Bonar.—C. M. D. *Spohr.*

Moderate. I heard the voice of Jes-us say: "Come un-to me and rest;

Lay down, thou wear-y one, lay down Thy head up-on my breast!"

I came to Jes-us as I was, Weary, and worn, and sad;

I found in him a rest-ing-place, And he hath made me glad.

[70]

130. Hymn 602.—Ellacombe.—C. M. D. *German.*

Cheerful. How hap - py ev - ry child of grace, Who knows his sins for - giv'n!

This earth, he cries, is not my place, I seek my place in heav'n:

A country far from mor - tal sight—Yet, O by faith I see

The land of rest, the saints' de - light, The heav'n prepar'd for me!

[71]

131.   Hymn 607.—Haydn.—C. M. Double.   *M. Hudyn.*

Cheerful. Jer - u - sa - lem, my hap - py home! Name ev - er dear to me!

When shall my la - bours have an end, in joy, and peace, and thee?

When shall these eyes thy heav'n-built walls And pear - ly gates be - hold?

Thy bulwarks with salvation strong, And streets of shining gold, And streets of shining gold?

[72]

132. Hymn 141.—St. Ursula.—C. M. D.   *F. Westlake.*

Cheerful. It came up-on the mid-night clear, That glorious song of   old,

From an-gels bend-ing   near   the earth to touch their harps of   gold;

"Peace   on   the earth, good-will   to men, From heav'n's all-gracious   King!"

The   world   in sol-emn   still-ness lay   To   hear   the an-gels sing.

END OF COMMON METRE TUNES.

[73]

133.

Hymn 652.—Bankfield.—S. M.

Hymnary.

Moderate. Hail to the Sab - bath day, The day di - vine - ly giv'n,

When men to God their hom - age pay, And earth draws near to heav'n.

134.

Hymn 662.—Bethel. —S. M.

Dr. Wesley.

Cheerful. Great is the Lord our God, And let his praise be great;

He makes his churches his a - bode, His most de - light - ful seat.

135. Hymn 233.—Boylston.—S. M. *Dr. Mason.*

Moderate. Make haste, O man, to live, For thou so soon must die;

Time hurries past thee like the breeze; How swift its moments fly!

136. Hymn 754.—Cambridge.—S. M. *Rev. R. Harrison.*

Moderate. Jes - us, we look to thee, Thy pro - mis'd presence claim!

Thou in the midst of us shalt be, As - sembled in thy name.

[75]

137.

Hymn 234.—Cana.—S. M.

C. W. Jordan.

Moderate. O where shall rest be found, Rest for the wea - ry soul?

'Twere vain the o - cean's depths to sound, Or seek from pole to pole.

138.

Hymn 198.—Carlisle.—S. M.

C. Lockhart.

Cheerful. Lord God, the Ho - ly Ghost, In this ac - cept - ed hour,

As on the day of Pen - te - cost, Descend in all thy pow'r

139.   **Hymn 661.—Christchurch,—S. M.**   *Dr. Wesley.*

Moderate.   I   love   thy   king - dom, Lord, The house . of   thine   a - bode,

The Church our blest Re - deem - er saves With his   own   pre - cious blood.

140.   **Hymn 758.—Dennis.—S. M.**   *H. G. Naegeli.*

Cheerful. Blest   be   the   tie   that binds, Our   hearts   in   Christian   love;

The   fel - low - ship of   kin - dred minds Is   like   to   that   a - bove.

[77]

Hymn 14.—Falcon Street.—S. M. *Isaac Smith.*

Bold. A - wake, and sing the song of Mo - ses and the Lamb;

Wake ev' - ry heart and ev' - ry tongue, To praise the Saviour's name.

DOXOLOGY.

Praise ye the Lord, Hal - le - lu - jah! Praise ye the Lord, Hal - le - lu - jah!

Hal - le - lu - jah! Hal - le - lu - jah! Hal - le - lu - jah! Praise ye the Lord!

142. **Hymn 496.—Franconia.—S. M.** *German.*

Slowly. "My times are in thy hand;" My God, I wish them there;

My life, my friends, my soul, I leave En-tire-ly to thy care.

143. **Hymn 753.—Leeds,—S. M.** *Sacred Harmony.*

Cheerful. And are we yet a-live, And see each o-ther's face?

Glo-ry and praise to Je-sus give For his redeem-ing grace!

[79]

144.

Hymn 684.—Mount Ephraim.—S. M.

Milgrove

Moderate. Lord of the har - vest, hear Thy nee - dy ser - vants' cry;

An - swer our faith's ef - fect - ual pray'r, And all our wants sup - ply.

145.

Hymn 248.—Potsdam.—S. M.

From Bach.

Moderate. O that I could re - pent, With all my i - dols part,

And to thy gracious eyes pre - sent A humble, con - trite heart!

[80]

146.   Hymn 16.—Prague.—S. M.   *Rev. L. R. West.*

Cheerful. Fa - ther, in whom we live, In whom we are, and move,

The glo - ry, pow'r, and praise re - ceive Of thy cre - a - ting love.

147.   Hymn 12.—Rhodes.—S. M.   *H. G. Trambeth.*

Cheerful. Come, sound his praise a - broad, And hymns of glo - ry sing;

Je - ho - vah is the sov'reign God, The u - ni - ver - sal King.

[81]

148. Hymn 13.—**Sabbath.**—S. M. *Swindells.*

Moderate. To God the on - ly wise, Our Sa - viour and our King,

Let all the saints be - low the skies Their humble prai - ses bring.

149. Hymn 854.—**Sarah.**—S. M. *W. Arnold.*

Moderate. And must this bo - dy die? This well - wrought frame de - cay?

And must these ac - tive limbs of mine Lie mould' - ring in the clay?

150. Hymn 462.—Serenity.—S. M. *C. Bryan.*

Cheerful. Who in the Lord con - fide, And feel his sprin - kl'd blood,

In storms and hur - ri - canes a - bide, Firm as the mount of God.

151. Hymn 157.—Shirland.—S. M. *Stanley.*

Moderate. Not all the blood of beasts On Jew - ish al - tars slain,

Could give the guil - ty conscience peace, Or wash a - way our stain.

[83]

152.

Hymn 247.—Supplication.—S. M.

Barnby.

Slowly. When shall thy love con-strain, And force me to thy breast?

When shall my soul re-turn a-gain To her e-ter-nal rest?

153.

Hymn 246.—St. Bride.—S. M.

Dr. Howard, 1762.

Slow. Ah! whither should I go, Burden'd, and sick, and faint!

To whom should I my troubles show, And pour out my com-plaint!

134.

1703.

Slowly. Mourn for the thou-sands slain, The youth-ful and the strong;

Mourn for the wine-cup's fear-ful reign, And the de-lu-ded throng.

155.

Hymn 403.—St. Helena.—S. M.

W. H. Monk.

Moderate. The pray-ing Spi-rit breathe, The watch-ing pow'r im-part;

From all en-tan-gle-ments be-neath Call off my anxious heart.

156.   Hymn 528.—St. Mary Redcliffe.—S. M.   *C. Bryan.*

Moderate. Blest are the pure in heart, For they shall see our God;

The sec - ret of the Lord is theirs, Their soul is his a - bode.

157.   Hymn 756.—St. Michael.—S. M.   *Day's Psalter, 1588.*

Moderate. Saviour of sin - ful men, Thy good - ness we pro - claim,

Which brings us here to meet a - gain, And triumph in thy name.

[86]

158. Hymn 526.—Thatcher.—S. M. *Handel.*

Moderate. Je - sus, my Truth, my Way, My sure, un - err - ing Light,

On thee my fee - ble steps I stay, Which thou wilt guide a - right.

159. Hymn 921.—Euxu.—S. M. *W. Mason.*

Moderate. We give thee but thine own, What - e'er the gift may be;

All that we have is thine a - lone, A trust, O Lord, from thee.

160. Hymn 247.—Warksworth,—S. M. *Foundery Collection, 1742.*

Moderate. When shall thy love con-strain, And force me to thy breast?

When shall my soul re-turn a-gain To her e-ter-nal rest?

161. Hymn 337.—Whitefield,—S. M. *E. Miller.*

Cheerful. Come, ye that love the Lord, And let your joys be known;

Join in a song with sweet ac-cord, While ye sur-round his throne.

[88]

162. Hymn 736.—Armageddon.—S. M. D. *Dr. Gauntlett.*

Bold. Lord, if at thy com - mand The word of life we sow,

Water'd by thy al - migh - ty hand, The seed shall sure - ly grow:

The vir - tue of thy grace A large in - crease shall give;

And mul - ti - ply the faith - ful race Who to thy glo - ry live.

[89]

163. **Hymn 454.—Diademata.—S. D.** *Sir G. J. Elvey.*

Bold. Sol - diers of Christ, a - rise! And put your ar - mour on;

Strong in the strength which God sup - plies Through his e - ter - nal Son;

Strong in the Lord of Hosts, And in his migh - ty pow'r,

Who in the strength of Je - sus trusts, Is more than con - quer - or.

164. Hymn .—Leomister.—S. M. D. *G. W. Martin.*

Slowly. A few more years shall roll, A few more sea - sons come,

And we shall be with those that rest, A - sleep with - in the tomb:

REFRAIN.

Then, O my Lord, pre - pare, My soul for that great day;

O wash me in thy pre - cious blood, And take my sins a - way

165. Hymn 615.—*Nearer Home.*—S. M. D.   *Isaac Woodbury.*

Moderate. "For - ev - er with the Lord!" A - men, so let it be!

Life from the dead is in that word, 'Tis im - mor - tal - i - ty.

Here in the bo - dy pent, Ab - sent from him I roam,

Yet night - ly pitch my mov - ing tent A day's march near - er home.

END OF SHORT METRE TUNES.

166. Hymn 374.—Adoration.—88, 88, 88. *Dodd.*

Bold. Great God of wonders! all thy ways Display the at - tributes di - vine; But countless acts of

pard'ning grace Be-yond thy other wonders shine, Beyond thy o - ther wonders shine.

CHORUS. Who is a pard'ning God like thee? Or who has grace so rich and free?

Who is a pard'ning God like thee? Or who has grace so rich and free?

[93]

167.   Hymn 297.—Bremen.—88, 88, 88.   *German.*

Moderate. Yes, from this in-stant now, I will To my of-fen-ded Fa-ther cry; My base in-gra-ti-tude I feel, Vi-lest of all thy chil-dren, I, Not wor-thy to be call'd thy son; Yet will I thee my Fa-ther own.

[94]

Hymn 264.—Brighton.—88, 88, 88.

Moderate. Fa - ther of Je - sus Christ, the Just, My Friend and

Ad - vo - cate with thee, Pi - ty a soul that fain would

trust In him who liv'd and died for me: But on - ly thou canst

make him known, And in my heart re - veal thy Son.

169. Hymn 730.—Calcutta.—88, 88, 88. H. B. Walmisley.

Cheerful. E - ter - nal Lord of earth and skies, We wait thy Spi - rit's

la - test call: Bid all our fall - en race a - rise,

Thou who hast purchas'd life for all; Whose on - ly name, to

sin - ners giv'n, Snatches from hell, and lifts to heav'n.

[96]

Hymn 16.—Castleton.—88, 88, 88.

Adam Wright.

Moderate. Lo! God is here! Let us a - dore, And own how dread - ful

is this place! Let all with - in us feel his pow'r, And

si - lent bow be - fore his face; Who know his pow'r, his

grace who prove, Serve him with awe, with rev'rence love.

G

[57]

171.

H. Lahee.

Moderate. Pris - 'ners of hope, be strong, be bold! Cast off your doubts, dis-

dain to fear! Dare to be - lieve; On Christ lay hold; Wres-

- tle with Christ in migh - ty pray'r; Tell him, "We will not

let thee go, Till we thy name, thy na - ture know."

172. **Hymn 190.—Colmar.—88, 88, 88.** *Michael Gasteritz.*

Cheerful. I want the Spirit of pow'r with - in, Of love, and
of a health - ful mind; Of pow'r, to con - quer in - brea
ain; Of love, to thee and all man - kind; Of health, that
pain and death de - fies, Most vigorous when the bo - dy dies.

[99]

173. Hymn 99.—Creation.—88, 88, 88. *F. J. Haydn.*

Bold. Far as cre - a - tion's bounds ex - tend, Thy mer - cies, heavenly

Lord, de - scend; One chorus of per - pet - ual praise, To thee thy

va - rious works shall raise; Thy saints to thee in

hymns im - part The trans - ports of a grate - ful heart.

174.   Hymn 488.—Eaton.—88, 88, 88.   Z. Wyvill.

Moderate. Sa - viour of all, what hast thou done, What hast thou suffer'd

on the tree! Why didst thou groan thy mor - tal groan, O -

- be - dient un - to death for me! The mystery of thy

pas - sion show, The end of all thy griefs be - low.

[101]

173.   **Hymn 381.—Euphony.—88, 88, 88.**   *T. Singleton.*

Cheerful.   Let God, who comforts the dis - trest, Let Is - rael's Con - so -

- la - tion hear! Hear, Holy Ghost, our joint re - quest, And show thy -

self the Com - fort - er; And swell th' un - ut - ter - a - ble groan,

And breathe our wish - es to the throne, And breathe our wish - es to the throne.

176.   **Hymn 486.—Giessen.—88, 88, 88.**

Moderate. When gath' - ring clouds a - round I view, And days are

dark, and friends are few, On him I lean, who not in

vain Ex - pe - rienc'd ev' - ry hu - man pain; He knows my

wants, al - lays my fears, And counts and treasures up my tears.

177. Hymn 488.—Maccabeus.—88, 88, 88. *Handel.*

Moderate. Sa - vi ur of all, what hast thou done, What hast thou suf - fer'd on the tree? Why didst thou groan thy mor - tal groan, O - be - dient un - to death for me? The mys - tery of thy pas - sion show, The end of all thy griefs be - low.

Hymn 933.—Melita.—88, 88, 88.   *Rev. Dr. Dykes.*

Moderate. E - ter - nal Fa - ther, strong to save, Whose arm doth bind the

rest - less wave, Who bidd'st the migh - ty o - cean deep Its

own ap - point - ed lim - its keep: O hear us when we

cry to thee For those in pe - ril on the sea!

Hymn 17.—Middlesex.—88, 88, 88.

Cheerful. My heart is fix'd, O God, my heart Is fix'd to tri-umph

in thy grace: (Awake, my lute, and bear a part:) My

glo - ry is to sing thy praise, Till all thy

na - ture I par - take, And bright in all thine im - age wake.

180.   Hymn 98.—Stella.—88, 88, 88.   *From "Crown of Jesus."*

Moderate.   Cap - tain of Israel's host, and Guide Of all who seek the

land a - bove, Be - neath thy sha - dow we a - bide, The

cloud of thy pro - tect - ing love: Our strength, thy

grace; our rule, thy word; Our end, the glo - ry of the Lord.

181.　　　　Hymn 731.—**Swaffham.**—88, 88, 88.　*Rev. G. P. Merrick, B.A.*

Lively. Lord o - ver all, if thou hast made, Hast ransom'd ev' - ry

soul of man, Why is the grace so long de - lay'd? Why

un - ful - fill'd the sav ing plan? The bliss, for A - dam's

race de - sign'd, When will it reach to all man - kind?

182.   Hymn 267.—St. Catherine.—88, 88, 88.

Moderate. Wea - ry of wan - d'ring from my God, And now made will - ing to re - turn, I hear and bow me to the rod; For thee, not without hope, I mourn: I have an Ad - vo - cate a - bove, A Friend be - fore the throne of Love.

Moderate. Peace! doubt - ing heart; my God's I am; Who form'd me man, for -

- bids my fear; The Lord hath call'd me by my name; The

Lord pro - tects, for ev - er near; His blood for me did

once a - tone, And still he loves and guards his own.

Hymn 549.—St. Paul.—88, 88, 88.   *T. W. Staniforth*

Bold. Pris - 'ners of hope, lift up your heads! The day of lib - er -

ty draws near; Je - sus, who on the ser - pent treads, Shall

soon in your be - half ap - pear; The Lord will to his

tem - ple come, Pre - pare your hearts to make him room.

185.　　　Hymn 20.—St. Werbergh.—88, 88, 88.　　　*Dr. Dykes.*

Moderate. My soul, in-spir'd with sa-cred love, The Lord thy God de-

-light to praise; His gifts I will for him im-prove, To

him de-vote my hap-py days; To him my thanks and

prais-es give, And on-ly for his glo-ry live.

186.   Hymn 613.—Valete.—88, 88, 88.   *Sir A. Sullivan.*

Moderate. Lead - er of faith - ful souls, and Guide Of all who trav - el

to the sky, Come, and with us, even us a - bide, Who

would on thee a - lone re - ly; On thee a - lone our

spi - rits stay, While held in life's un - e - ven way.

H   [113]

Hymn 423.—Bradford.—888, 888. *(2nd Metre).*   *Wm. Horsley.*

Moderate. Thou, Je - sus, thou my breast in - spire, And touch my

lips with hal - low'd fire, And loose thy stamm'ring servant's tongue:

Pre - pare the ves - sel of thy grace; A - dorn me

with the robes of praise, And mer - cy shall be all my song.

188. **Hymn 61.—Brunswick Chapel.—888, 888.** *(2nd Metre.)* *Beresford.*

Cheerful. Fa - ther of ev - er - last - ing grace, Thy good - ness

and thy truth we praise, Thy good - ness and thy truth we prove;

Thou hast, in hon - our of thy Son, The gift un - speak - a -

- ble sent down, The Spirit of life, and pow'r, and love.

[115]

189. Hymn 62.—Centennial.—888, 888. *(2nd Metre.)* *J. H. Paine.*

Moderate. I'll praise my Mak - er while I've breath, And when my

voice is lost in death, Praise shall em - ploy my no - bler powers;

My days of praise shall ne'er be past, While life, and thought, and

be - ing last, Or im - mor - tal - i - ty en - dures.

192. Hymn 681.—Zurich.—888, 888. *(2nd Metre.)* *Swiss Melody.*

Moderate. O Je - sus, source of calm re - pose, Thy like nor man nor

an - gel knows; Fair - est a - mong ten thous - and fair.

Even those whom death's sad fet - ters bound, Whom thick - est darkness

com - pass'd round, Find light and life, if thou ap - pear.

[119]

Hymn 880.—Acclamation.—66, 66, 88.

Cheerful. Ye vir - gin souls, a - rise! With all the

dead a - wake! Un - to sal - va - tion wise, Oil

in your ves - sels take; Up - start - ing at the

mid - night cry: "Be - hold the heav'n - ly Bridegroom nigh!"

194.   **Hymn 178.—Bevan.—66, 66, 88.**   *Sir John Goss.*

Cheerful. God is gone up on high, With a tri - um - phant

noise; The clar - ions of the sky Pro - claim the' an-

gel - ic - joys! Join all on earth, re -

joice and sing; Glo - ry as - cribe to glo - ry's King.

195. **Hymn 737.—Caledon.—66, 66, 88.** *Weigh House Chapel Coll.*

Moderate. Saviour, we know thou art In ev - 'ry age the same; Now, Lord, in ours ex - ert The

virtue of thy name; And daily, thro' thy word, increase Thy blood-besprinkl'd wit - ness - es.

196. **Hymn 657.—Darwell.—66, 66, 88.** *Rev. J. Darwell.*

Cheerful. Lord of the worlds a - bove, How pleasant and how fair The dwellings of thy

love, Thy earth - ly tem - ples are! To thine a - bode my

heart as - pires, With warm de - sires, to see my God.

197.   Hymn 211.—Jubilee.—66, 66, 88.   *P. C. Chatlock.*

Bold. Blow ye the trumpet, blow, The glad - ly sol - emn sound:

Let all the na - tions know, To earth's re - mot - est bound,

The year of Ju - bi - lee is come: Re - turn, ye ransom'd sinners, home.

198.

Moderate. Ye vir - gin souls, a - rise! With all the dead a - wake! Un-

to sal - va - tion wise, Oil in your ves - sels take: Up - start - ing

at the mid - night cry, "Be - hold the heav'nly Bridegroom nigh!"

199.

R. C. Trampleasure.

Moderate. Awake, ye saints, awake! And hail this sacred day ; In loftiest songs of praise Your joyful

[124]

homage pay; Come, bless the day that God hath blest, The type of heav'n's e-ter-nal rest.

200.   **Hymn 122.—Samuel.—66, 66, 88.**   *Sir Arthur Sullivan.*

Moderate.   A - rise, my soul, a - rise! Shake off thy guil - ty fears;

The bleed - ing Sac - ri - fice In my be - half ap - pears:

Be - fore the throne my Sure - ty stands, My name is writ - ten on his hands.

[125]

201.

Hymn 891.—Southampton.—66, 66, 88.

Dr. Arnold.

Cheerful. The Lord of earth and sky, The God of a - ges praise;

Who reigns en - thron'd on high, An - cient of end - less days:

Who lengthens out our tri - al here, And spares us yet a - no - ther year.

202.

Hymn 119.—Steggall.—66, 66, 88.

Dr. Steggall.

Cheerful. Let earth and heav'n a - gree, Angels and men be join'd, To cel - e - brate with me The

Steggall—*Continued.*

Saviour of mankind; To' a - dore the all-atoning Lamb. And bless the sound of Je - sus' name.

203.   Hymn 676.—**St. Swithin.**—66, 66, 88.   *E. Jesser.*

Moderate.   Great King of glo - ry, come, And with thy fa - vour crown This

tem - ple as thy home, This peo - ple as thine own; Be - neath this

roof O deign to show How God can dwell with men be - low!

[127]

204. Hymn 115.—Ariel.—886, 886. *Dr. L. Mason.*

Cheerful. O could I speak the match-less worth, O

could I sound the glo-ries forth, Which in my Sa-viour shine,

I'd soar and touch the heav'nly strings, And vie with Ga-briel

while he sings In notes almost di-vine, In notes al-most di-vine.

[128]

Moderate. Light of the world thy beams I bless! On thee, bright

Sun of Righteous ness, My faith hath fix'd its eye;

Guid - ed by thee, through all I go, Nor fear the

ru - in spread be - low, For thou art al - ways nigh.

206.

Hymn 450.—Ynspruck,—886, 886.

H. Isaac.

Moderate. Help, Lord, to whom for help I fly, And still my tempt - ed

soul stand by Through - out the ev - il day;

The sac - red watch - ful - ness im - part, And keep the is - sues

of my heart, And stir me up to pray.

[130]

207. Hymn 586.—Jonn.—886. 886. *Sir G. Smart.*

Moderate. Sa - viour, on me the want be - stow, Which all that feel shall

sure - ly know: Their sins on earth for - giv'n.

Give me to prove the king - dom mine, And taste, in ho - li -

- ness di - vine, The hap - pi - ness of heav'n.

[131]

Hymn 584.—Magdalen College.—886, 886. *Dr. Wm. Hayes.*

Moderate. O Love Di - vine, how sweet thou art! When shall I find my

will - ing heart All ta - ken up by thee?

I thirst, I faint, I die to prove The greatness of re -

- deem - ing love, The love of Christ to me!

209. **Hymn 37.—Maudesley Street.—886, 886.**

Cheerful. O thou to whom arch - an - gels raise A cease - less song of

per - fect praise, Yet trem - ble as they sing; To

us in - cline thy gra - cious ear, And while, with rev'rence,

we draw near, Ac - cept the praise we bring, Ac - cept the praise we bring.

[133]

210.   Hymn 288.—𝕸eribah.—886, 886.   *Dr. Mason.*

Moderate. Thou great mys-ter-ious God un-known, Whose love hath gent-

-ly led me on, Even from my in-fant days: Mine

in-most soul ex-pose to view, And tell me, if

I ev-er knew Thy jus-ti-fy-ing grace.

[134]

211.   Hymn 290.—Pembroke.—886, 886.   *J. Foster.*

Moderate. Thee, Je - sus, thee, the sin - ner's Friend, I fol - low
on to ap - pre - hend, Re - new the glorious strife;
Di - vine - ly con - fi - dent and bold, With faith's strong
arm on thee lay hold, Thee, my e - ter - nal life.

[135]

212.

Hymn 35.—Purleigh.—886, 886.

A. H. Brown.

Moderate. O that I could, in ev' - ry place, By faith behold Je - hovah's face; My

strict Ob - serv - er see Pres - ent, my heart and reins to try; And

feel the influence of his eye For ev - er fix'd on me!

213.

Hymn 801.—Hungerford.—559, 559.

Dr. Gauntlett.

Cheerful. A - way with our fears! The glad morning appears, When an heir of sal - va - tion was born!

[136]

Hungerford—*Continued.*

From Jehov-ah I came, For his glo-ry I am, And to him I with singing re-turn.

214.   **Hymn 353.—Stour Valley.—559, 559.**   *Dr. Gauntlett.*

Cheerful. O how hap-py are we Who in Je - sus a - gree To ex -

- pect his re - turn from a - bove! We sit un - der our Vine, And de-

- light - ful - ly join In the praise of his ex - cel - lent love.

[157]

215.

Hymn 162.—Harwich.—5.5.11, 5.5.11.

M'grove.

Slowly. All ye that pass by, To Jesus draw nigh: To you is it

nothing that Jesus should die! Your ransom and peace, Your

Saviour he is; Come, see if there ever was sorrow like his.

216.

Hymn 892.—Derbe.—5.5.5, 11.

Sacred Harmony.

Cheerful. Come, let us anew, Our journey pursue,

Derbe—*Continued.*

Roll round with the year, Roll round with the year, And

nev - er stand still, And nev - er stand still till the Mas - ter ap - pear.

217.   **Hymn 630.—Sherbrook.—5.5.5, 11.**

Cheerful. Come, let us a - new, Our jour - ney pur - sue,

With vig - our a - rise, And press to our per - manent place in the skies.

[139]

Hymn 399.—Bethany.—6.4, 6.4, 6.6.4.

Dr. L. Mason.

Moderate. Near - er, my God, to thee, Near - er to thee! E'en though it

be a cross That raiseth me! Still all my song shall be, Near - er, my

God, to thee, Nearer, my God, to thee, Near - er to thee.

Hymn 398.—Love.—6.4, 6.4, 6.6.4.

Moderate. More love to thee, O Christ, More love to thee; Here thou the pray'r I make, On bend - ed knee; This is my ear - nest plea,

More love, O Christ, to thee, More love, O Christ, to thee, More love to thee.

220. **Hymn 399.—Sullivan.—6.4, 6.4, 6.6.4.** *Sir Arthur Sullivan.*

Slowly. Nearer, my God, to thee, Nearer to thee; E'en tho' it be a cross that rais - eth me,

Still all my song shall be, Nearer, my God, to thee, Near - er to thee, Nearer to thee.

221. Hymn 746.—Onward.—6.5, 6.5, 6.5, 6.5. *Sir Arthur Sullivan.*

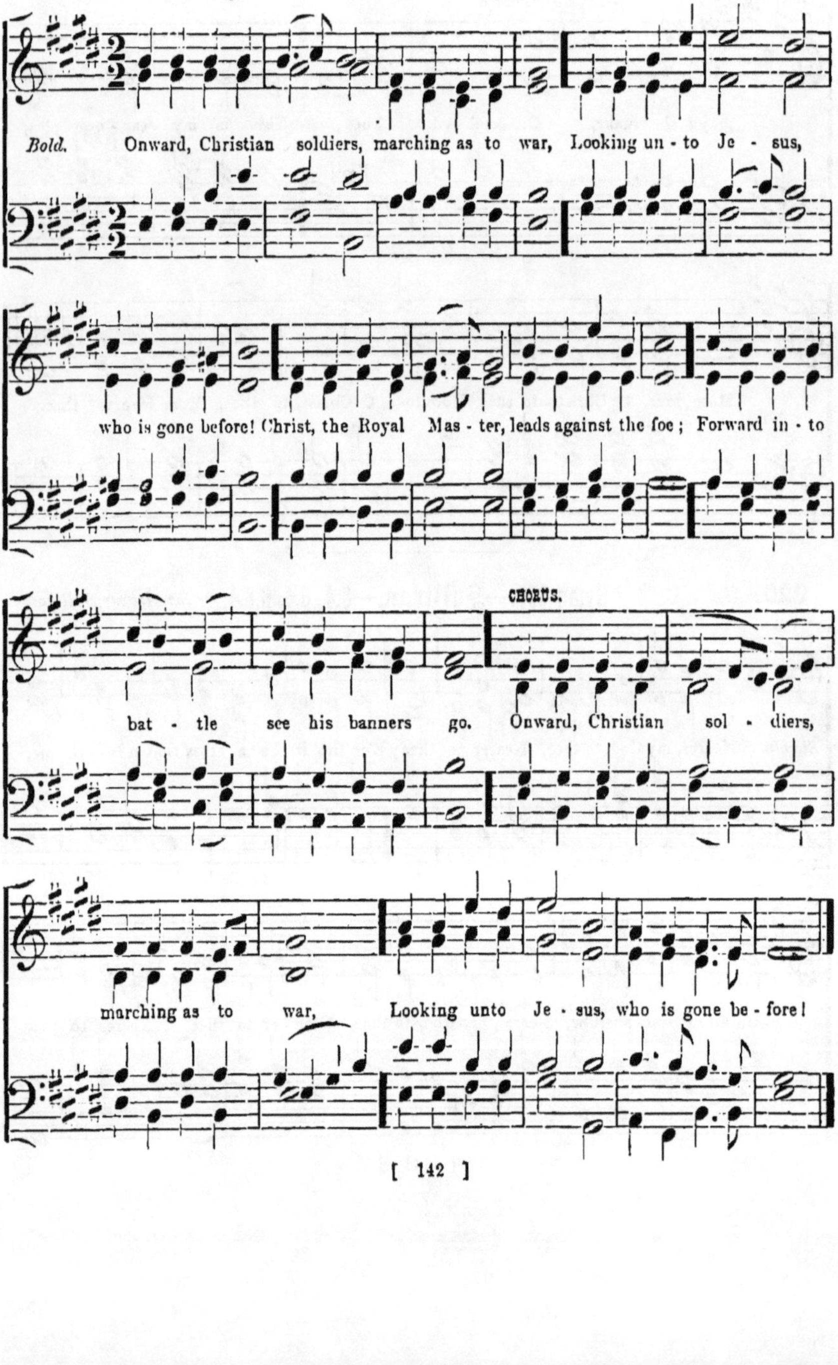

222. Hymn 862.—"*Lowly and Solemn be.*"—6.6.4, 6.6.4. *E. L. White.*

Slowly. Low-ly and sol-emn be Thy children's cry to thee, Fa-ther di-vine!

A hymn of suppliant breath, Own-ing that life and death A-like are thine.

223. Hymn 903.—**Canada.**—6.6.4, 6.6.6.4. *Dr. L. Mason.*

Boldly God bless our native land! Firm may she ever stand, Thro' storm and night; When the wild

tempests rave, Rul-er of wind and wave, Do thou our country save By thy great might!

[157]

224. **Hymn 904.—"God Save the Queen."—6.6.4, 6.6.6.4.**

Boldly. God save our gracious Queen, Long live our noble Queen, God save the Queen; Send her vic-

to - ri - ous, Happy and glo - rious, Long to reign o - ver us; God save the Queen.

225. **Hymn 27.—Italian Hymn.—6.6.4, 6.6.6.4.** *F. Giardini.*

Moderate. Come, thou Al - mighty King, Help us thy name to sing; Help us to praise! Father all

glo - ri - ous; O'er all vic - to - ri - ous, Come and reign o - ver us, Ancient of days.

226.   Hymn 26.—Newhaven.—6.6.4, 6.6.6.4.   *Dr. T. Hastings.*

Thou whose Al - mighty Word Cha - os and darkness heard, And took their flight; Hear us, we

Moderate.

humbly pray, And where the gospel-day Sheds not its glorious ray. Let there be light!

227.   Hymn 400.—Olivet.—6.6.4, 6.6.6.4.   *Dr L. Mason.*

Slowly. My faith looks up to thee, Thou Lamb of Cal - va - ry, Saviour di - vine: Now

hear me while I pray; Take all my sins a - way; O let me from this day Be wholly thine

228.   Hymn 501.—*Fiducia.*—6.6, 6.6.   St. Albans' Tune Book.

Slowly Thy way, not mine, O Lord, How-ev-er dark it be!

Lead me by thine own hand, Choose out the path for me.

229.   Hymn 779.—*Lomas.*—6.6, 6.6, 6.6.   G. Lomas.

Slowly. I gave my life for thee, My precious blood I shed, That thou might'st ransom'd

be, And quicken'd from the dead. I gave my life for thee; What hast thou done for me?

[146]

230.   Hymn 501.—*Sheba.*—6.6, 6.6, 6.6, 6.6.   *Rev. W. H. Havergal.*

Slowly. Thy way, not mine, O Lord, How - ev - er dark it be:

Lead me by thine own hand, Choose out the path for me;

Smooth let it be or rough, It still will be the best,

Wind ing or straight, it leads Right on - ward to thy rest.

[147]

231. **Hymn 125.—Eccles.—6.6, 7.7, 7.7.** *Boggett.*

Moderate. A - rise, my soul, a - rise, Thy Sa - viour's sac - ri - fice!

All the names that love could find, All the forms that love could take,

Je - sus in him - self hath join'd, Thee, my soul, his

own to make, Thee, my soul, his own to make.

[148]

232. Hymn 69.—*Fulneck.*—6.6, 7.7, 7.7. *Rev. C. L. Latrobe*

Moderate. Hail, co - es - sen - tial Three, In mys - tic

Un - i - ty! Fa - ther, Son, and Spi - rit,

hail! God by heav'n and earth a - dor'd, God in -

in thy glo - ries blest, With God Mes - si - ah ev - er reign!

233.　　　Hymn 199.—**Thornton.**—6.6, 7.7, 7.7.　　　*F. Hiller.*

Moderate. E - ter - nal Spi - rit, come In - to thy mean - est home:

From thy high and ho - ly place, Where thou dost in glo - ry reign,

Stoop, in con - de - scending grace, Stoop to the poor heart of man.

own to make, Thee, my soul, his own to make.

[148]

237. Hymn 39.—Harvington.—6.6.8.4, 6.6.8.4.   *A. E. Kette.*

Moderate. Though na - ture's strength de - cay, And earth and hell with -

235. Hymn 124.—Hilary.—6.6.8, 6.6.8.   *Marot and Beza's Psalms.*

Lively. Je - ru - sa - lem di - vine, When shall I call thee mine? And to thy

ho - ly hill at - tain, Where wea - ry pil - grims rest, And

in thy glo - ries blest, With God Mes - si - ah ev - er reign!

[151]

233.　　　　　　Hymn 199.—Thornton.—6.6, 7.7, 7.7.　　　*F. Hiller.*

Moderate. E - ter - nal Spi - rit, come In - to thy mean - est home:

call thee mine? And to thy ho - ly hill at - tain,

Where wea - ry pil - grims rest, And in thy glo - ries

blest, With God Mes - si - ah ev - er reign?

[152]

237. Hymn 39.—**Harrington.**—6.6.8.4, 6.6.8.4.   *A. E. Kettle.*

Moderate. Though na - ture's strength de - cay, And earth and hell with -

- stand, To Canaan's bounds I urge my way, At his com - mand.

The wa - t'ry deep I pass, With Je - sus in my

view; And through the howl - ing wil - der - ness My way pur - sue.

Hymn 38.—Leoni.—6.6.8.4, 6.6.8.4.

Jewish Melody.

Moderate. The God of Abraham praise, Who reigns enthron'd a - bove, An - cient of ev - er-

-last - ing days, And God of love Je - ho - vah, Great I AM, By

earth and heav'n con - fest; I bow and bless the sa - cred Name, For ev - er blest.

Hymn 861.—Bath.—6.6, 8.6, 8.8.

W. H. Cooke.

Slow. Friend after friend departs; Who hath not lost a friend? There is no union here of hearts

That finds not here an end; Were this frail world our only rest, Living or dy - ing, none were blest.

240. Hymn 861.—Lucca.—6.6, 8.6, 8 8. *J. H. Schein*

Slow. Friend af - ter friend de - parts, Who hath not lost a friend?

There is no u - nion here of hearts, That finds not here an end.

Were this frail world our on - ly rest, Liv - ing or dy - ing, none were blest.

[155]

241.

Hymn 126.—**Aurelia.**—7.6, 7.6, 7.6, 7.6.

Dr. S. S. Wesley.

Moderate. O Lamb of God! still keep me Near to thy wounded side;

'Tis on - ly there in safe - ty And peace I can a - bide.

What foes and snares sur - round me! What lust and fears with - in!

The grace that sought and found me A - lone can keep me clean.

242.

Hymn 621.—Ewing.—7.6, 7.6, 7.6, 7.6   *Alexander Ewing.*

Cheerful. Je - ru - sa - lem the gold - en ! with milk and hon - ey blest,

Be - neath thy con - tem - pla - tion Sink heart and voice op - prest;

I know not, O I know not What so - cial joys are there!

What ra - dian - cy of glo - ry, What light be - yond com - pare.

[157]

243. **Hymn 908.—Lancashire.—7.6,7.6,7.6,7.6.** *Sir Henry Smart.*

Lively. Sing to the Lord of har-vest! Sing songs of love and praise!

With joy-ful hearts and voi-ces Your Hal-le-lu-jahs raise;

By him the roll-ing seas-ons in fruit-ful or-der move;

Sing to the Lord of har-vest A song of hap-py love.

[153]

244. Hymn 744.—Missionary.—7.6, 7.6, 7.6, 7.6. *Dr. L. Mason.*

Moderate. From Greenland's i - cy moun - tains, From In - dia's cor - al strand,

Where Af - ric's sun - ny foun - tains Roll down their gol - den sand,

From ma - ny an an - cient riv - er, From ma - ny a palm - y plain,

They call us to de - liv - er Their land from err - or's chain.

[159]

245. **Hymn 743.—Morning Light.—7.6, 7.6, 7.6, 7.6.** *G. J. Webb.*

Moderate. The morn - ing light is break - ing; The dark - ness dis - ap - pears;

The sons of earth are wak - ing To pen - i - ten - tial tears:

Each breeze that sweeps the o - cean Brings tid - ings from a - far,

Of na - tions in com - mo - tion, Pre - par'd for Zi - on's war.

[160]

Slowly. I need thee, pre - cious Je - sus! For I am full of sin;

My soul is dark and guil - ty, My heart is dead with - in:

I need the cleansing foun - tain, Where I can al - ways flee—

The blood of Christ most pre - cious, The sin - ner's per - fect plea.

Hymn 721.—St. Theodulph.—7.6, 7.6, 7.6, 7.6. *Melchior Teschner.*

Lively. Hail to the Lord's An · oint · ed, Great Da · vid's great · er Son!

Hail, in the time ap · point · ed, His reign on earth be · gun!

He comes to break op · pression, To let the cap · tive free,

To take a · way trans · gres · sion, And rule in e · qui · ty.

248. Hymn 57.—Asylum.—7.6, 7.6, 7.7, 7.6. *T. Clark.*

Moderate. Meet and right it is to sing, In ev-'ry time and place,

Glo-ry to our heavenly King, The God of truth and grace:

Join we then with sweet ac-cord, All in one thanksgiving join,

Holy, ho-ly, holy, Lord, E-ter-nal praise be thine, E-ternal praise be thine!

249. Hymn 504.—**Cowley.**—7.6, 7.6, 7.7, 7.6. *Walmisley.*

Moderate. O Almigh - ty God of Love, Thy ho - ly arm dis - play;

Send me suc - cour from a - bove, In this my e - vil day;

Arm my weakness with thy pow'r, Light of life, ap - pear with - in;

Be my Safeguard and my Tower A - gainst the face of sin.

[164]

250. Hymn 149.—*Faith.*—7.6, 7.6, 7.7, 7.6. *Dr. S. S. Wesley.*

Moderate. Cel - e - brate Im - manuel's name, The Prince of Life and Peace;

God with us, our lips pro - claim, Our faithful hearts con - fess:

God is in our flesh re - veal'd Earth and heav'n in Je - sus join;

Mor - tal with im - mor - tal fill'd And hu - man with di - vine.

[165]

251. Hymn 150.—Galt —7.6, 7.6, 7.7, 7.6.   *G. D. Wilson.*

Moderate. God of un - ex - ampl'd grace, Re - deem - er of man - kind,

Mat - ter of e - ter - nal praise We in thy pas - sion find:

Still our choic - est strains we bring, Still the joy - ful theme pur - sue,

Thee the Friend of sin - ners sing, Whose love is ev - er new.

[166]

252. Hymn 415.—St. Hilary—7.6, 7.6, 7.7, 7.6. *Rev. Dr. Dykes.*

Moderate. Father of our dy-ing Lord, Re-mem-ber us for good;

O ful-fil his faith-ful word, And heat his speak-ing blood!

Give us that for which he prays; Fa-ther, glo-ri-fy thy Son!

Show his truth, and pow'r, and grace, And send the pro-mise down.

Hymn 331.—Amsterdam.—7.6, 7.6, 7.8, 7.6.

Dr. Nares.

Moderate. Je - sus, take my sins a - way, And make me know thy name;

Thou art now, as yes - ter - day And ev - er - more, the same.

Thou my true Beth - es - da be; I know with - in thine arms is room;

All the world may un - to thee, Their House of Mer - cy, come.

254. **Hymn 317.—Falkirk.—7.6, 7.6, 7.8, 7.6.** *T. A. Arne.*

Slowly. Let the world their vir-tue boast, Their works of righteous-ness;

I, a wretch un-done and lost, Am free-ly sav'd by grace:

O-ther ti-tle I disclaim; This, on-ly this, is all my plea:

I the chief of sin-ners am, But Je-sus died for me.

Hymn 435.—Gilead.—7.6, 7.6, 7,8 ,7.6.

Sir H. S. Oakeley.

Lively. Lo! I come with joy to do The Mas-ter's bless-ed will;

Him in out-ward works pur-sue, And serve his plea-sure still.

Faith-ful to my Lord's commands, I still would choose the bet-ter part;

Serve with care-ful Mar-tha's hands, And lov-ing Ma-ry's heart.

256. Hymn 543.—Josiah.—7.6, 7.6, 7.8, 7.6. *W. Arnold.*

Cheerful. None is like Je - shurun's God, So great, so strong, so high, Lo! he

spreads his wings abroad, He rides up - on the sky; Is - rael is his first-born son;

God, the Almigh - ty God. is thine; See him to thy help come down. The

excellence di - vine; See him to thy help come down, The ex - cellence di - vine.

[171]

257. Hymn 413.—Russell Place.—7.6, 7.6, 7.8, 7.6. *Sir W. S. Bennett.*

Moderate. Come, ye followers of the Lord, In Jesus' service join,

Jesus gives the sacred word, The ordinance divine:

Let us his command obey, And ask and have whate'er we want:

Pray we, ev'ry moment pray, And never, never faint.

[172]

258. Hymn 812.—St. Antolius.—7.6, 7.6, 8.8. *A. H. Brown.*

Moderate. The day is past and o - ver; All

thanks, O Lord, to thee! We pray thee now that sin - less The

hours of night may be; O Je - sus, keep us

in thy sight, And save us through the com - ing night!

[173]

259. Hymn 812.—Twilight—7.6, 7.6, 8.8. *Joseph Barnby.*

Lively. The day is past and o-ver; All thanks, O
Lord, to thee, We pray thee now that sin-less
thee, We pray . . . .
The hours of dark may be: O Je-sus, keep us
be: O Je-sus keep us
in thy sight,
in thy sight, And save us through the com - ing night.

[174]

260. Hymn 204—**Comfort.**—7 7.7. *Sir A. Sullivan.*

Slow Ho - ly Ghost! my Com - fort - er! Now from

high - est heav'n ap - pear, Shed thy gra - cious radiance here.

261. Hymn 204.—**St. Philip.**—7.7.7. *W. H. Monk.*

Slow Ho - ly Ghost! my Com - fort - er! Now from high - est

heav'n ap - pear, Shed thy gra - cious ra - diance here.

262.　　　Hymn 177.—Ascension.—7.7.7.7.　　　S. Reay.

Lively. Hail the day that sees him rise, Hal - le - lu - jah!

To his throne a - bove the skies, Hal - le - lu - jah!

Christ the Lamb for sin - ners giv'n, Hal - le - lu - jah!

En - ters now the high - est heav'n, Hal . . . . le - lu - jah!

263.   Hymn 594.—Ashford,—7.7 7.7   *C. H. Rink.*

Moderate. Ho - ly Lamb, who thee re - ceive, Who in thee be - gin to live,

Day and night they cry to thee, As thou art, so let us be!

264.   Hymn 770.—Christ Chapel.—7.7.7.7.   *Dr. Steggall.*

Moderate. When this song of praise shall cease Let thy chil - dren, Lord, de - part

With the bless - ing of thy peace, And thy love in ev - ry heart.

M   177

265. Hymn 740.—**Clarion.**—7.7.7.7. *Dr. Rimbault*

Briskly. Earth, re - joice, our Lord is King! Sons of men, his prais - es sing!

Sing ye in tri - um - phant strains, Je - sus the Mes - si - ah reigns!

266. Hymn 174.—**Easter Hymn.**—7.7.7.7. *Carey.*

Cheerful. "Christ, the Lord, is ris'n to - day," Hal . . . . . . le - lu - jah!

Sons of men and an - gels say, Hal . . . . . . le - lu - jah!

[17]

Easter Hymn.—*Continued.*

Raise your joys and triumphs high, Hal - - - - - - le - - - lu - - jah!

Sing, ye heav'ns thou earth re - ply, Hal - - - - - - - le - - lu - jah!

267. Hymn 176—Essex.—7 7 7 7. *Thomas Clarke.*

Lively. Christ, the Lord, is ris'n a - gain, Christ hath broken ev - 'ry chain; Hark! angel - ic

voi - ces cry, Singing ev - er - more on high: Hal - le - lu - jah! Praise the Lord!

[179]

263.   Hymn 655.—**German Hymn.**—7.7.7.7.   *Pleyel.*

Moderate. Soft-ly fades the twi-light ray Of the ho-ly Sab-bath day;

Gent-ly as life's set-ting sun, When the Christian's course is run.

269.   Hymn 217.—**Barrow.**—7.7.7.7.   *Rev. F. A. J. Hervey.*

Slowly. Brother, hast thou wander'd far From thy Father's hap-py home,

With thy-self and God at war! Turn thee, brother; home-ward come.

[180]

270.

Hymn 161.—Holley—7.7 7.7.

G. Hews.

Moderate. Nev - er further than thy cross, Nev - er high - er than thy feet;

Here earth's precious things seem dross; Here earth's bit - ter things grow sweet.

271.

Hymn 675.—Innocents.—7.7.7.7.

Arranged by W. H. Monk.

Moderate. Lord of hosts! to thee we raise Here a house of pray'r and praise;

Thou thy peo - ple's hearts pre - pare, Here to meet for praise and pray'r.

272.

Hymn 502.—Judah.—7 7.7.7.

J. V. Watts.

Moderate. As thy day thy strength shall be— This should be e - nough for thee;

He who knows thy frame will spare Burdens more than thou canst bear.

273.

Hymn 824.—Mariner's.—7.7.7.7.

Moderate. God the Fa - ther! be thou near, - - - -

Save from ev - 'ry harm to - night;

[182]

Mariner's.—*Continued.*

Make us all thy chil - dren dear,

In the dark - ness be our light.

274.   **Hymn 196.—Mercy.—7 7 7.7.**   *L. M. Gottschalk.*

Slowly. Gra - cious Spi - rit, Love di - vine, Let thy light with - in me shine!

All my guil - ty fears re - move; Fill me with thy heav'nly love.

[183]

275. **Hymn 177.—Nuremberg.—7.7.7.7.**

Lively. Hail the day that sees him rise To his throne a - bove the skies;

Christ the Lamb for sin - ners giv'n, En - ters now the high - est heav'n.

---

276. **Hymn 409.—Prayer.—7 7.7.7.** *A Abbott*

Slowly. Father, at thy footstool see Those who now are one in thee

Draw us by thy grace a - lone, Give, O give us to thy Son!

277.

Hymn 245.—Putney.—7.7.7.7.

Rev. Wm Blow.

Slowly. Ho - ly Spi - rit ! pi - ty me, Pierc'd with grief for griev - ing thee ;

Present, though I mourn a - part, Listen to a wail - ing heart.

278.

Hymn 503.—Redhead.—7.7.7.7.

R. Redhead.

Slowly. When our heads are bow'd with woe, When our bit - ter tears o'erflow,

When we mourn the lost, the dear, Je - sus, Son of Da - vid, hear.

[185]

279. Hymn 197.—**Seymour.**—7.7.7 7. *C. M. Von Weber.*

Slowly. Ho - ly Ghost, with light di - vine, Shine up - on this heart of mine;

Chase the shades of night a - way Turn my dark - ness in - to day.

280. Hymn 160.—**Ajalon.**—7.7, 7.7, 7.7. *R. Redhead.*

Slow. Rock of A - ges, cleft for me, Let me hide my - self in thee;

Let the wa - ter and the blood, From thy wounded side which flow'd,

Ajalon.—*Continued.*

Be of sin the double cure, Save from wrath and make me pure.

---

281.   Hymn 882.—**Celano.**—7.7, 7.7, 7.7.

Slow.   Day of wrath, O dreadful day! When this world shall pass a - way.

And the heav'ns to - geth - er roll, Shriv'ling like a parch - ed scroll,

Long fore - saint and sage. Psalmist's harp, and prophet's page.

282.　Hymn 195.—Crowland.—7.7, 7.7, 7.7.　*Johann Schop.*

Moderate. Fa - ther, glo - ri - fy thy Son, An - swer - ing his all -

- pow'r - ful pray'r; Send the In - ter - ces - sor down,

Send that oth - er Com - fort - er, Whom be - liev - ing -

- ly we claim, Whom we ask in Je - sus' name.

[188]

283.

Hymn 275.—Dix.—7.7, 7.7, 7.7.

C. Kocher.

Moderate. Why not now, my God, my God? Rea-dy if thou al-ways art, Make in me thy mean a-bode, Take pos-ses-sion of my heart; If thou canst so great-ly bow. Friend of sin-ners, why not now?

[189]

284.

Lively. As with glad . ness men of old Did the guid - ing

star be - hold ; As with joy they hail'd its light,

Lead - ing on - ward, beam - ing bright ; So, most gra - cious

Lord, iv we Ev - er - more be led to thee.

285. Hymn 270.—Nassau.—7.7, 7.7, 7.7. *J. Rosenmuller.*

Moderate. Christ, whose glo - ry fills the skies, Christ, the true, the
on - ly Light, Sun of Righteous - ness, a - rise,
Tri - umph o'er the shades of night; Day - spring from on
high, be near, Day - star, in my heart ap - pear.

Hymn 646.—Sabbath.—7.7, 7.7, 7.7.

Dr. L. Mason.

Cheerful. Safe - ly through an - o - ther week, God has brought us on our way;

Let us now a blessing seek, Waiting in his courts to - day:

Day of all the week the best, Em - blem of e - ter - nal rest,

Day of all the week the best, Em - blem of e - ter - nal rest.

Hymn 274.—Seville.—7.7, 7.7, 7.7.

Spanish Chant.

Moderate.

Je - sus, Shep - herd of the sheep, Pi - ty my un -
-set - tl'd soul! Guide, and nour - ish me, and keep,
Till thy love shall make me whole: Give me per - fect.
sound - ness, give; Make me stead - fast - ly be - lieve.

288. **Hymn 273.—Temple.—7.7, 7.7, 7.7.** E. J. Hopkins.

Moderate.

Sav - iour, Prince of Is - rael's race, See me from thy
lof - ty throne; Give the sweet re - lent - ing grace
Soft - en this ob - dur - ate stone; Stone to flesh, O
God, con - vert! Cast a look, and break my heart.

[194]

289.   Hymn 222.—Wells.—7.7, 7 7, 7.7.   *D. Bortnianski.*

Moderate. Wea - ry souls, that wan - der wide From the cen - tral

point of bliss, Turn to Je - sus cru - ci - fied,

Fly to those dear wounds of his: Sink in - to the

pur - ple flood; Rise in - to the life of God.

[195]

Hymn 741.—"Hark! the Song."—7.7, 7.7, 7.7, 7.7.   *F. Weber.*

Cheerful. Hark! the song of ju - bi - lee; Loud as migh - ty thunders roar,

Or the ful - ness of the sea, When it breaks up - on the shore:

Hal - le - lu - jah! for the Lord God Om - ni - po - tent shall reign·

Hal - le - lu - jah! let the word Ech - o round the earth and main.

291. Hymn 117.—**Kollingside.**—7.7, 7.7, 7.7, 7.7. *Rev. Dr. Dykes.*

Moderate. Je - sus, Lov - er of my soul Let me to thy bo - som fly,

While the near - er wa - ters roll, While the tem - pest still is high:

Hide me, O my Saviour, hide, Till the storm of life be past;

Safe in - to the ha - ven guide O re - ceive my soul at last!

[197]

292. Hymn 243.—Maidstone.—7.7, 7.7, 7.7, 7.7. *W. B. Gilbert.*

Moderate. Depth of mer - cy, can there be Mer - cy still reserv'd for me?

Can my God his wrath for - bear? Me, the chief of sinners, spare?

I have long with - stood his grace, Long pro vok'd him to his face

Would not hearken to his calls, Griev'd him by a thousand falls

293.   Hymn 142.—**Mendelssohn.**—7.7, 7.7, 7.7, 7.7.   *F. B. Mendelssohn.*

Boldly. Hark! the her - ald - an - gels sing: "Glory to the new-born King; Peace on earth and

mercy mild, God and sin - ners recon - cil'd." Joyful, all ye nations, rise,

Join the triumph of the skies; With an - gelic hosts proclaim "Christ is born in

Bethlehem!" Hark! the herald - angels sing: "Glo - ry to the new-born King!"

ORGAN PED.

[199]

294.

Sir G. Elvey.

Cheerful. Come, ye thankful peo-ple, come, Raise the song of harvest-home;

All is safe-ly gather'd in, Ere the win-ter storms be-gin:

God, our Mak-er doth pro-vide For our wants to be sup-plied;

Come to God's own tem-ple, come, Raise the song of har-vest-home!

295. Hymn 691.—Thanksgiving.—7.7, 7.7, 7.7, 7.7. *Wm. Gilbert.*

Lively. Light of Life, ser - a - phic fire, Love Di - vine, thy - self im - part;

Ev - 'ry fainting soul in - spire, Shine in ev - 'ry drooping heart.

Ev - 'ry mournful sin - ner cheer, Scat - ter all our guil - ty gloom;

Son of God, ap - pear, ap - pear, To thy human temples come!

296.

Slowly. Sa - viour, when in dust to thee Low we bow th' a - dor - ing knee:

When, re - pent - ant, to the skies Scarce we lift our weeping eyes,

O, by all thy pains and woe, Suffer'd once for man be - low,

Bend - ing from thy throne on high, Hear our sol - emn li - ta - ny.

297. Hymn 218.—Requies.—7.7, 7.7, 7.7, 7.7.   *Blumenthal.*

Slowly. Come, ye wea - ry sin - ners, come All who groan be - neath your load;

Je - sus calls his wand'rers home Hast en to your pard'ning God!

Come, ye guil - ty spirits, op - press'd. Answer to the Saviour's call:

"Come, and I will give you rest; Come, and I will save you all.'

[203]

Hymn 473.—Grasmere.—7.7, 8.7, 7.7, 8.7. *Edwin Moss.*

Lively. Head of thy church tri - um - phant We joy - ful - ly a - dore thee;

Till thou appear, Thy members here Shall sing like those in glo - ry.

We lift our hearts and voi - ces With blest an - ti - ci - pa - tion,

And cry aloud, And give to God The praise of our sal - va - tion.

Hymn 473.—Protomartyr.—7.7, 8.7, 7.7, 8.7. *Dr. Gauntlett.*

Lively.

Head of thy church tri - umphant, We joy - ful - ly a - dore thee;

Till thou ap - pear, Thy members here Shall sing like those in glo - ry.

We lift our hearts and voi - ces With blest an - ti - ci - pa - tion,

And cry a - loud, And give to God The praise of our sal - va - tion.

300.   **Hymn 474.—Worship.—7.7, 8.7, 7.7, 8.7.**   *Michael Haydn.*

Cheerful. Wor - ship, and thanks, and bless - ing, And strength ascribe to Je - sus!

Je - sus a - lone de - fends his own, When earth and hell op - press us.

Je - sus with joy we wit ness Al - migh - ty to de - liv - er;

Our seals set to, that God is true, And reigns a King for ev - er.

[206]

301. Hymn 857.—"Vital Spark."—7.7, 8.8, 7.7. (Irregular). *Adapted.*

Slowly.

Vi - tal spark of heav'n - ly flame! Quit, oh, quit this

mor - tal frame; Trem bling, hope - ing, ling - ring, fly - ing,

O the pain, the bliss of dying! Cease, fond na - ture,

cease thy strife, And let me lan - guish in - to life!

[207]

302.
Hymn 858.—"The Long Home."—7.8, 7.8, 7.7. *Sir A. Sullivan.*

Slowly. Ten - der Shep - herd, thou hast still'd Now thy lit - tle lamb's brief weep ing; Ah, how peace - ful, pale, and mild, In its nar - row bed 'tis sleep - ing! And no sigh of an - guish sore Heaves that lit - tle bos - om more.

303.   Hymn 213.—"Art thou Weary?"—8.5, 8.3.   *E. W. Bullinger.*

Slowly.   Art thou wea-ry,   hea-vy-lad-en?   Art thou   sore dis-trest?

"Come to me," saith One "and com-ing.   Be   at   rest."

304.   Hymn 775.—Rest.—8.5, 8.3.   *Sir A. Sullivan.*

Slowly   I am trust-ing thee. Lord Je-sus,   Trusting on-ly   thee;

Trust-ing thee for full sal-va-tion, Great and   free.

[209]

305. **Hymn 622.—Paradise.—8.6, 8.6, 8.6, 6.6.** *Sir Henry Smart.*

Moderate. O Par - a - dise! O - Par - a - dise! Who doth not crave for rest?

Who would not seek the hap - py land Where they that lov'd are blest;

Where loy - al hearts and true Stand ev - er in the light,

All rap - ture through and through, In God's most ho - ly sight'

[210]

306. **Hymn 622.—Rapture.—8.6, 8.6, 6.6, 6.6.**   *J. Barnby.*

Moderate. O Par - a - dise! O Par - a - dise! Who doth not crave for rest

Who would not seek the hap - py land Where they that lov'd are blest;

Where loy - al hearts and true Stand ev - er in the light,

All rap - ture through and through In God's most ho - ly sight!

[211]

307.

J. H. Cornell.

Moderate. Ho - ly Ghost, dis - pel our sad - ness, Pierce the

clouds of Na - ture's night; Come, thou Source of joy and

glad - ness, Breathe thy life, and spread thy light.

308.

Hymn 225.—Newton Ferns.—8.7, 8.7.

Samuel Smith.

Moderate. There's a wide - ness in God's mer - cy, Like the wide - ness of the sea;

[212]

Newton Ferns.—*Continued.*

There's a kindness in his jus - tice, Which is more than lib - er - ty.

309. Hymn 168.—**Vermont.**—8.7, 8.7. *Weber.*

Moderate. Sweet the mo - ments, rich in bless - ing, Which be -

- fore the cross I spend; Life, and health, and

peace pos - sess - ing, From the sin - ner's dy - ing Friend.

[213]

310.   Hymn 877.—Calvary.—8.7, 8.7, 4.7.   *Stanley*

Moderate. Lift your heads, ye friends of Je - sus, Part - ners in his sufferings here;

Christ to all be - liev - ers precious, Lord of lords shall soon ap - pear;

Mark the to - kens, Mark the to - kens Of his heavenly kingdom near!

---

311.   Hymn 145 —Christmas.—8.7, 8.7, 4.7.   *W. T. H. Alchin.*

Cheerful. Angels, from the realms of glo - ry. Wing your flight o er all the earth Yo who sang creation's sto - ry,

[214]

Christmas.—*Continued.*

312. Hymn 879.—Helmsley.—8.7, 8.7, 4.7. *From "Lock Collection."*

313.   Hymn 175.—Regent's Square.—8.7, 8.7, 4.7.   *Sir H. Smart.*

Cheerful. Come, ye saints, look here and won - der, See the

place where Je - sus lay; He has burst his bands a - sun - der; He has

borne our sins a - way; Joy - ful tid - ings! Joy - ful

tid - ings! Yes, the Lord has ris'n to - day.

314. Hymn 922.—St. Thomas.—8.7, 8.7, 4.7. *Vincent Novello.*

Moderate. Now, O Lord, ful - fil thy pleas - ure; Breathe up - on thy

chos - en band; And, with pen - te - cos - tal meas - ure,

Send forth reap - ers o'er our land— Faith - ful reap - ers,

Faith - ful reap - ers, Gathering sheaves for thy right hand.

[217]

315.   Hymn 28.—St. Raphael.—8.7, 8.7, 4.7.   *E. J. Hopkins.*

Cheerful. God the Lord is King; be - fore him,

Earth, with all thy na - tions. wait! Where the cher - u -

bim a - dore him. Sit - teth he in roy - al state;

He is ho - ly, Bless - ed, on - ly Po - ten - tate!

316. Hymn 666.—Triumph.—8. 7, 8. 7, 4 7.   *Dr. Gauntlett.*

Bold. Zi - on stands with hills sur - round - ed, Zi - on, kept by

pow'r di - vine; All her foes shall be con - found - ed,

Though the world in arms com - bine; Hap - py Zi - on,

Hap - py Zi - on, What a fa - vour'd lot is thine!

[219]

317.

Hymn 506.—Worms.—8.7, 8.7, 6.6, 6.7.   *Martin Luther.*

Boldly. A mighty for·tress is our God, A bulwark nev·er fail·ing;

Our help·er he, a·mid the flood Of mortal ills pre·vail·ing.

For still our an·cient foe Doth seek to work us woe;

His craft and pow'r are great, And, arm'd with cruel hate, On earth is not his e·qual.

318.   Hymn 825.—Evensong.—8.7, 8.7, 7.7.   *J. Summers.*

Moderate. Through the day thy love hath spar'd us; Wea - ried we lie

down to rest; Through the si - lent watch - es guard us,

Let no foe our peace mo - lest; Je - sus, thou our

Guar - dian be, Sweet it is to trust in thee.

[221]

319.

Hymn 825.—Gounod.—8.7, 8.7, 7.7.

C. Gounod.

Moderate. Thro' the day thy love hath spar'd us; Wearied we lie down to rest; Thro' the silent watches guard us,

Let no foe our peace molest; Jesus, thou our Guardian be, Sweet it is to trust in thee.

320.

Hymn 434.—Zurich.—8.7, 8.7, 7.7.

S. Schop, 1640.

Moderate. Join'd to Christ in mys-tic un-ion— We thy mem-bers, thou our Head—

Seal'd by deep and true com-mun-ion, Ris'n with thee, who once were dead—

Zurich.—*Continued.*

Sav - iour, we would hum - bly claim All the pow'r of this thy name.

321. **Hymn 664.—Austria.—8.7, 8.7, 8.7, 8.7.** *Haydn, 1809.*

Bold. { Glorious things of thee are spo - ken. Zi - on, ci - ty of our God; }
{ He, whose word can - not be bro - ken. Form'd thee for his own a - bode; }

On the Rock of A - ges found ed, What can shake thy sure re - pose!

With salvation's walls surrounded, Thou may'st smile at all thy foes.

[223]

322.   Doxology 12.—Benediction.—8.7, 8.7, 8.7, 8.7.   *S. Webbs.*

Moderate. Lord, dis - miss us with thy blessing, Bid us now de - part in peace;

Still on heavenly man - na feed - ing, Let our faith and love in - crease;

Fill each breast with conso - lation; Up to thee our hearts we raise; When we reach yon

blissful station, Then we'll give thee no - bler praise! Halle - lu - jah! Halle - lu - jah!

[224]

323. Hymn 144.— **Granta.**—8.7, 8.7, 8.7, 8.7. *Dr. T. A. Walmisley.*

Cheerful. Come, thou long-ex - pect - ed Je - sus, Born to set thy peo - ple free,

From our fears and sins re - lease us, Let us find our rest in thee.

Is - rael's strength and con - so - la - tion, Hope of all the earth thou art;

Dear De - sire of ev' - ry nation, Joy of ev' - ry longing heart.

·P   [225]

Hymn 31.—Mant.—8.7, 8.7, 8.7, 8.7.

Sir A. Sullivan.

Cheerful. Praise the Lord! ye heav'ns, a - dore him; Praise him, an - gels, in the height;

Sun and moon, re - joice be - fore him; Praise him, all ye stars of light;

Praise the Lord! for he hath spok - en, Worlds his migh - ty voice o - bey'd;

Laws, that nev - er shall be broken, For their guidance he hath made.

325.   Hymn 476.—Salvator.—8.7, 8.7, 8.7, 8.7.   *J. P. Judson.*

Moderate. Lord of life, when foes assail us And our hearts are bow'd in pain,

Earth - ly friends can not de - liv - er; Swords and bucklers, all are vain.

Be our Buckler, thou whose pi - ty Bore the shame up - on the **tree;**

Man of Sorrows! in our sorrows We can on - ly trust in thee.

326. Hymn 436.—Toronto.—8.7, 8.7, 8.7, 8.7. *Sir A. Sullivan.*

Cheerful. Hark, the voice of Je - sus call - ing, "Who will go and work to - day?

Fields are white, and harvests wait - ing, Who will bear the sheaves a - way?"

Loud and long the Mas - ter call - eth, Rich re - ward he of - fers free;

Who will an - swer, glad - ly say - ing, "Here am I, O Lord, send me?"

327. Hymn 169.—*Tribute.*—8.7, 8.7, 8.7, 8.7.   *Sir H. Smart.*

Cheerful. In the cross of Christ I glo - ry, Tow'ring o'er the wrecks of time;

All the light of sa - cred sto - ry Ga - thers round its head sublime.

When the woes of life o'ertake me, Hopes de - ceive, and fears an - noy,

Nev - er shall the cross for - sake me; Still it glows with peace and joy.

[229]

328.   Hymn 881.—**Luther's Hymn.**—8.7, 8.7, 8.8.7.   *Martin Luther.*

Boldly.   Great God! what do I see and hear! The end of things cre-

-a - ted! The Judge of man I see ap - pear, On

clouds of glo - ry seat - ed: The trumpet sounds, the graves restore The

dead which they contained before: Pre - pare, my soul, to meet him!

[230]

Slowly. Dark - ly rose the guil - ty morn - ing, When, the King of

Glo - ry scorn - ing, Rag'd the fierce Jer - u - sa - lem;

See the Christ, his cross up - bear - ing, See him strick - en,

wound - ed, wear - ing The thorn - platt - ed di - a - dem.

330.   Hymn 205.—"Living Water."—8.8,7.7.   *German.*

Moderate. Liv - ing Wa - ter, free - ly flow - ing, Fount of gladness, life be - stow - ing,

Ho - ly Spi - rit, O draw nigh, While thy name we mag - ni - fy!

331.   Hymn 500.—Elm Street.—8 8. 8 4.   *Dr Dykes.*

Moderate. My God, and Fa - ther, while I stray Far from my home, in life's rough way,

O teach me from my heart to say, Thy will be done!

[232]

332. **Hymn 253.—Southport.—8.8 8 4**   *G Lomas.*

Moderate. Je - sus, my Sa - viour, look on me, For I am weary and opprest;

I come to cast my - self on thee. Thou art my Rest.

333. **Hymn 255.—"Agnus Dei."—8.8, 8.6.**   *Rev. Wm. Blow.*

Slowly Just as I am, without one plea But that thy blood was shed for me,

And that thou bidd'st me come to thee, O Lamb of God, I come!

[233]

334.   Hymn 255.—Woodworth.—8.8, 8.6.   *W. B. Bradbury.*

Slowly. Just as I am, with-out one plea, But that thy blood was shed for me,

And that thou bidd'st me come to thee, O Lamb of God, I come! I come!

---

335.   Hymn 254.—Wyedale.—8.8, 8.6.   *Rev. W. H. Havergal.*

Moderate. Just as thou art, with-out one trace Of love, or joy, or in-ward grace,

Or meetness for the heav'n-ly place, O guil-ty sin-ner, come!

336.

Moderate. Thou Shepherd of Is - rael, and mine, The joy and de - sire of my heart,

For clo - ser com - mun - ion I pine. I long to re side where thou art:

The pasture I languish to find, Where all who their Shepherd o - bey

Are fed, on thy bo - som re - clin'd, And screen'd from the heat of the day.

337.   Hymn 628.—Sion.—8.8, 8.8, 8.8, 8.8.   *Sacred Harmony.*

Cheerful. A - way with our sor - row and fear! We soon shall re - cov - er our home;

The ci - ty of saints shall ap - pear, The day of e - ter - ni - ty come:

From earth we shall quick - ly re - move, And mount to our na - tive a - bode,

The house of our Fa - ther a - bove, The pal - ace of an - gels and God.

338.   Hymn 864.—Madison.—8.8, 8.8. (Double).

Moderate. O when shall we sweet-ly re-move, O when shall we en-ter our rest,

Re-turn to the Zi-on a-bove, The mo-ther of spir-its distrest

339.   Hymn 314.—St. David's.—8.8, 8.8. (Double).   *Handel.*

Moderate. How shall a lost sin-ner in pain Re-cov-er his for-feit-ed peace?

When brought in-to bond-age a-gain, What hope of a sec-ond re-lease?

[237]

340.

Hymn 705.—Cheddon.—9.8, 9.8.

Sullivan's Collection.

Moderate. Bread of the world, in mer-cy broken! Wine of the soul, in mer-cy shed!

By whom the words of life were spo-ken, And in whose death our sins are dead.

341.

Hymn 705.—Gotha.—9.8, 9.8.

H.R.H. the late Prince Consort.

Moderate. Bread of the world, in mer-cy broken! Wine of the soul, in mer-cy shed!

By whom the words of life were spoken, And in whose death our sins are dead.

342. Hymn 97.—Lux Benigna.—10.4, 10.4, 10.10. *Rev. J. B. Dykes.*

Moderate. Lead, kind - ly light, amid th'en - circling gloom, Lead thou me on. - - -

The night is dark, and I am far from home; Lead thou me on. - -

Keep thou my feet; I do not ask to see - - - - -

The dis - tant scene; one step e - nough for me.

[239]

343. **Hymn 783.—Cecilia.—10.10, 10.10.** *Adapted from Filby.*

Lively. Singing for Je-sus, our Saviour and King, Singing for Je-sus, the Lord whom we love;

All a-dor-a-tion we joy-ous-ly bring, Longing to praise as we'll praise him a-bove.

344. **Hymn 656.—Ellerton.—10.10, 10.10.** *J. Barnby.*

Moderate. Sa-viour, a-gain to thy dear name we raise,

With one ac-cord, our parting hymn of praise; We stand to bless thee

[240]

ere our worship cease, Then, low - ly kneeling, wait thy word of peace.

345. **Hymn 784.—Eventide.—10.10, 10.10.** *W. H. Monk.*

Moderate. A - bide with me, fast falls the ev - en - tide ; The dark - ness

deep - ens ; Lord, with me a - bide ! When oth - er help - ers

fail, and comforts flee, Help of the helpless, O a - bide with me !

Q

313. Hymn 784.—Toulon.—10.10, 10.10. *C. Goudimel.*

Moderate. A - bide with me, fast falls the even - tide; The darkness deepens, Lord, with me a-bide!

When other help - ers fail, and comforts flee. Help of the helpless, O a - bide with me!

347. Hymn 349.—Beethoven—10.10, 11.11. *L. Beethoven*

Cheerful. O heav - en - ly King, look down from a - bove! As - sist us to

sing thy mer - cy and love; So sweet - ly o'er - flow - ing, so

Beethoven.—*Continued.*

plenteous the store, Thou art still be - stowing, and giv - ing us more.

---

348.   Hymn 786 —**Hanover.**—10 10, 11.11.   *Handel.*

Moderate.   Ap - pointed by thee, we meet in thy name, And meek - ly a-

gree to fol - low the Lamb, To trace thy ex - am - ple, the

world to dis - dain, And constant ly tram - ple on pleasure and pain.

349. **Hymn 29.—Houghton.—10.10, 11.11.** *Dr. Gauntlett.*

Modera'e. O worship the King all glorious a - bove! O gratefully sing his pow'r and his love!

Our Shield and De - fender, the Ancient of Days, Pavilion'd in splendour, and girded with praise.

350. **Hymn 351.—Jesmond.—10.12, 10.12.** *Dr. Dykes.*

Lively. My God, I am thine! what a com - fort divine, What a bless - ing to

know that my Je - sus is mine! In the heaven - ly Lamb thrice

[211]

Jesmond.—*Continued.*

hap - py I am, And my heart it doth dance at the sound of his name.

---

351.   Hymn 351.—Kingswood.—10.12, 10.12.   *Wallhead.*

Moderate. My God, I am thine! what a comfort di - vine, What a blessing to

know that my Je - sus is mine! In the heaven - ly Lamb thrice

hap - py I am, And my heart it doth dance at the sound of his name.

[245]

352. **Hymn 70—Goderich.—11.8, 11.8.** *W. H. W. Darley.*

Cheerful. Be joy-ful in God, all ye lands of the earth; O serve him with

glad-ness and fear! Ex-ult in his presence with mus-ic and

mirth, With love and de-votion draw near, With love and de-vo-tion draw near.

353. **Hymn 214—"Come, ye Disconsolate."—11.10, 11.10.** *Webbe.*

Slowly Come, ye dis-con-so-late, wher-e'er ye lan-guish; Come to the

[246]

mer - cy - seat, fer - vent - ly kneel; Here bring your wounded hearts,

here tell your anguish; Earth has no sorrow that Heav'n cannot heal.

354. **Hymn 146.—Epiphany.—11.10, 11.10.** *Rev. J. F. Thrupp.*

Moderate. Brightest and best of the sons of the morning, Dawn on our darkness and lend us thine aid;

Star of the East, the hor - i - zon adorning, Guide where our infant Redeemer is laid.

[247]

Hymn 479.—Portuguese Hymn.—11,11,11,11.   *J Reading*

Cheerful. How firm a found - a - tion, ye saints of the Lord, Is laid for your

faith in his ex - cel - lent word! What more can he say, than to

you he hath said, To you, who for ref - uge to Je - sus have

fled? To you, who for ref - uge to Je - sus have fled.

356. Hymn 24.—*Nicæa.*—11,13,12,10. *Dr. Dykes.*

Boldly. Ho - ly, ho - ly, ho - ly, Lord God Al - migh - ty!

Grate - ful - ly a - dor - ing our song shall rise to thee;

Ho - ly, ho - ly, ho - ly, mer - ci - ful and migh - ty,

God in Three Per - sons, bless - ed Trin - i - ty!

[249]

Boldly. Ho - ly, holy, ho - ly, Lord God Al - migh - ty!

Grate - ful - ly a - dor - ing our song shall rise to thee;

Ho - ly, ho - ly, ho - ly, mer - ci - ful and migh - ty,

God in Three Per - sons, bless - ed Trin - i - ty!

Hymn 865.—Cms —13,11,13,12.   *German Chorale.*

Slow. Thou art gone to the grave, but we will not de - plore thee,

Though sor - rows and dark - ness en - com - pass the tomb;

Thy Sa - viour has pass'd thro' its por - tal be - fore thee,

And the lamp of his love is thy guide thro' the gloom.

CHANTS AND SENTENCES.

Chant 15.—"Te Deum Laudamus."

Sir F. A. G. Ousley.

J. Battishill.

J. Robinson.

359.—I.

360.—II.

361.—III.

1	We praise	...	...	thee,	O	God;
3	To thee all Angels	...	...	cry	a	loud;
5	Holy	...	...	ho - ly,	ho - ly,	
7	The glorious company of the Apostles	...	praise	thee;		
9	The Holy Church, throughout all the world doth ac	knowledge	Glory,	O	Christ;	
11	Thou art the King of	...	sharpness of	death		
13	When thou tookst overcome the	...	be our	Judge		
15	We believe that thou shalt come to	...	bless thine			
17	O Lord, save thy people, and	...	safe,	O Lord		
19	Vouch	...	lighten up	on us,		
21	O Lord, let thy mercy	...				

we acknowledge ...	he	the
the heavens, and ...	powers there -	Lord,
Lord	to	in -
The goodly fellowship of the	the	oth :
the Father of an ...	praise	thee :
thou art the ever	un - mite	ty,
thou must open the kingdom of	Son of the	Father.
we therefore pray thee, help thy servants, whom	all be -	lievers.
govern them, and	lift them	blood.
to keep us this	day with -	ever.
as our	trust is	in ... thee.

"Te Deum Laudamus."—*Continued*

2. All the earth doth	wor - ship	thee,	the	Fa - ther	ev - er -	lasting.
4. To thee Cherubim, and	Ser - a -	phim	con-	tinu - al -	ly do	cry :
6. Heaven and	earth are	full	of the	majes ty	of thy	Glory.
8. The	no - ble	army	of	Mar - tyrs	praise	thee.
10. Thine adorable, true, and	on - ly	Son,	also the	Ho - ly	Ghost, the	Comforter.
12. When thou tookest upon thee to de-	liv - er	man,	thou didst humble thyself to be	born	of a	virgin.
14. Thou sittest at the right	hand of	God,	in the	glo - ry	of the	Father.
16. Make them to be numbered	with thy	saints,	in	glo - ry	ev - er -	lasting.
18. Day by day we	magni - fy	thee ;	and we worship thy	name, ever,	worldwithout	end.
20. O Lord, have	mercy up-	on us,	have	mer - cy	up - on	us.
22. O Lord, in	thee have I	trusted,	let me	nev - er	be con -	founded.

362.

Doxology 19.—"Gloria in Excelsis."

Arranged by W. H. W. Darley.

1. Glory be to .. :: .. :: God on high,
2. We praise thee, we bless thee, we :: wor - ship thee

and on earth
we glorify thee, we give thanks to :: ::

peace, good-
thee for

will toward
thy great

men.
glory.

3. O Lord God, .. :: .. heaven - ly King,
4. O Lord, the only begotten Son, .. :: Jo - sus

God the
O Lord God, lamb of God,

Fa - ther
Son ::

Al- .. :: the
of .. :: Father.

mighty,
the

5. That takest away the :: :: :: sins of the world,
6. Thou that takest away the :: :: :: sins of the world,
7. Thou that takest away the :: :: sins of the God
8. Thou that sittest at the right hand of :: God the Father,

have
have
re- ..
have

mercy up-
mercy up-
ceive ::
mercy up-

on
on
our
on

us.
us.
prayer.
us.

9. For thou only :: .. :: holy; thou
10. Thou only, O Christ, with the :: :: Ho - ly Ghost,

art .. :: holy;
art most high in the ::

on - ly
glory of

art the
God, the

Lord
Father.

A - men.

A - men.

[254]

Doxology 18.—Psalm lxvii.

From Spohr

363.—I.

1 God be merciful unto
3 Let the people
5 Let the people
8 Glory be to the Father and

us and
praise thee, O
praise thee, O
to the

and shew us the light of his countenance, and be ..
yea, let ..
yea, let ..
and ..

mer - ci -
all the
all the
to the

ful un -
peo - ple
peo - ple
Ho - ly

to us.
praise thee
praise thee
Ghost.

364.—II. *Morning Tune.*

2 That thy way may be
4 O let the nations rejoice ..
6 Then shall the earth bring
9 As it was in the beginning is now and

known upon earth.
and be glad
forth her
ev - er

thy saving
for thou shalt judge the people righteously, and
govern the
and God even our own ..
and all the ends of the
world with

health a -
na - tions
God, shall
world shall
out end

mong all
up on earth
give us his blessing
fear ..
A ..

nations.
give us his blessing
him.
Amen

255]

365. Baptismal Chant.—16.

Tullis.

1. And Jesus said, Suffer little children, and forbid them not to .. .. .. come unto me; .. For of such .. .. .. is the .. kingdom of heaven.
2. He shall feed his flock, ... like a .. shep-herd: He shall gather the lambs with his arm, and carry them in his bosom.
3. I will pour my Spirit upon thy seed, and my blessing up.. .. .. on thine .. .. off-spring: And they shall spring up as among the grass, as willows by the water-courses.
4. Go ye, therefore, and teach all nations, baptizing them into the name of the Father, and of the Son, and of the { Holy Ghost; { Teaching them to observe all things whatsoever I have commanded you, and lo! I am with you always, even .. .. unto .. .. of the world. Amen.
5. Glory be to the Father, and to the Son, and to the { Holy Ghost; As it was in the beginning, is now, and ever shall be .. world with-out .. end, Amen

366. Doxology 17.—"The Strain Upraise."—Irregular.

A. H. D. Troyte.

1. The strain upraise of joy and praise, Alle- In .. .. In dwell To the glory of their King Shall the ransomed Shall re-echo pro ple sing thro the sky Alle- .. .. lu .. ia, A - men.
2. And the choirs that dwell on high Paradise who dwell
3. They in the rest of heavenly way
4. The planets beaming on their heavenly way The blessed ones, with joy the .. cho - rus swell, The shining constellations join, and say lu .. .. ia, A - men.
5. Ye clouds that onward sweep Ye thunders echoing loud and deep, Ye lightnings wild-ly bright Alle- lu .. .. ia, A - men.
6. Ye storms and winter snow, Ye days of cloudless beauty summer glow, Your unto .. .. lu .. .. ia, A - men.
7. First let the birds, with painted plumage gay Exalt their great Creator's Your Alle- In sweet con- sent unite Ye groves that wave in spring And gratious lu .. .. ia, A - men.
8. Then let the beasts of earth, with varying strain, Join in creation's hymn, and cry a - gain. Alle- lu .. .. ia, A - men.
9. Here let the mountains thunder forth so- nor - ous, There let the valleys sing in gentler Alle- Ye tracts of earth and cont cho .. rus, lu .. .. ia, A - men.
10. Thou jubilant abyss of o - cean cry Alle- ments reply, du - ly paid. lu .. .. ia, A - men.
11. To God, who all cre- a - tion made, The frequent hymn be { This is the song, the heavenly strain, the Lord All- King approves; lu .. .. ia, A - men.
12. Wherefore we sing, both heart and voice, a- mighty loves: And chil-dren's voices echo. answer mak- ing In .. .. ia, A - men.
13. Now from all men .. .. wak - - ing, be outpoured With Alleluia to the Lord; The ever- more er - er- In .. .. ia, A - men.
14. To men .. .. be outpoured The Son and Spirit In .. .. ia, A - men.
15. Praise be done to the Three in One. Alle- lu .. .. ia, A - men.

367. Hymn 928. *Sir G. Elvey.*

Strong Son of God, im - mor - tal Love, Whom we, that have not seen thy face,

By faith, and faith a - lone, em - brace, Believing where we cannot prove.

368. Hymn 384.

From every stormy wind that blows, From every swelling tide of woes,

There is a calm, a sure retreat, 'Tis found beneath the mer - cy - seat.

369. **Hymn 9.** *A. Sharp.*

From all that dwell be - low the skies Let the Cre - a - tor's praise a - rise;

Let the Redeemer's name be sung, Through every land, by ev - ry tongue.

370. **Hymn 636.** *Robinson.*

Come, Holy Ghost, our hearts in spire, Let us thine influence prove;

Source of the old pro - phet - ic fire, Foun - tain of Light and Love.

[258]

Hymn 559.

For ever here my rest shall be, Close to thy bleeding side;

This all my hope, and all my plea, For me the Saviour died!

Hymn 925.

Father supreme, by whom we live, Thou who art God a - lone,

Our songs of grateful praise re - ceive, And make our hearts thy throne.

373.   **Hymn 1.**   *James Shaw*

O for a thousand tongues to sing My great Re - deem - er's praise,

The glories of my God and King, The triumphs of his grace!

---

374.   **Hymn 255.**   *Dixon.*

Just as I am, with - out one plea But that thy blood was shed for me,

And that thou bidd'st me come to thee, O Lamb of God, I come!

375.   **Hymn 500.**   *A. D. H. Troyte.*

My God and Father, while I stray Far from my home, in life's rough way,

O teach me from my heart to say, Thy will be done!

376.   **Hymn 632.**   *L T. Downes.*

One sweetly sol - emn thought Comes to me o'er and o'er,—

I am nearer home to day Than I ever have been be - fore.

377.—I.

Sanctus.

Camidge.

Ho - ly, Ho - ly, Ho - ly, Lord God of hosts! Heav'n and earth are

full of thy glo - ry: glo - ry be to thee. O Lord Most High.

378.—II.

Sanctus.

Thomas Ebdon.

Ho - ly, Ho - ly, Ho - ly, Lord God, Lord God of hosts! Heav'n and earth are

glory be to thee,

full of thy glo - ry; glo - ry be to thee, O Lord Most High.

379. **Trisagion.**

Holy, holy, holy Lord God of Sabaoth; heaven and earth are full.. .. of thy glory Hosanna in the highest: Blessed is he that cometh in the name of the Lord, Ho- sanna in the highest.

Tersanctus.

Therefore, with angels and arch angels, and with all the company of .. heaven, We laud and magnify thy glorious name.

Evermore praising thee, and say-ing, Ho-ly, Ho-ly, Ho-ly, Lord God of Hosts:

Heav'n and earth are full of thy glo-ry, Glo-ry be to thee, O Lord Most High. Amen.

[263]

OLD MELODIES.

380. Hymn 419.—Hebron.—L. M. *Dr. L. Mason.*

Forth in thy name, O Lord, I go, My dai-ly la-bour to pursue,

Thee, on-ly thee, re-solv'd to know, In all I think, or speak, or do.

381. Hymn 192.—Migdol.—L. M. *Dr. L. Mason.*

Father, if just-ly still we claim To us and ours the pro-mise made,

To us be graciously the same, And crown with liv-ing fire our head.

382. **Hymn 258.—Russia.—L. M.** *Billings.*

Lord, I de - spair myself to heal; I see my sin, but can - not feel; { I cannot till, I cannot
cannot, till thy Spirit

till thy Spirit blow, And bid th' obedient waters flow, } And bid th' obedient wa - - ters flow.
blow, and bid th' obedient wa - - - ters flow. . . .

383. **Hymn 709.—Uxbridge.—L. M.** *Dr. L. Mason.*

The heav'ns declare thy glo - ry, Lord, In ev - ry star thy wis - dom shines;

But when our eyes behold thy Word, We read thy name in fair - er lines.

[255]

384.

Bradbury

When, gracious Lord, when shall it be, That I shall find my all in thee!

The fulness of thy pro - mise prove, The seal of thine e - ter - nal love!

385.

Hymn 111.—Antioch.—C. M.

From Handel.

Joy to the world! the Lord is come; Let earth re-

- ceive her King; Let ev - ry heart pre - pare him room,

[266]

Antioch.—*Continued.*

And heav'n and na - ture sing, And heav'n and na - ture

And heav'n - - - And heav'n and na - ture sing, - - - And

sing, - - And heav'n, And heav'n and na - ture sing

heav'n and na - ture sing.

386.   Hymn 472.—**Arlington.**—C. M.   *Arne.*

Am I a sol - dier of the cross, A follower of the Lamb,

And shall I fear to own his cause, Or blush to speak his name?

[267]

387.

Hymn 108.—Coronation.—C. M.

All hail the pow'r of Jesus' name! Let angels prostrate fall;

Bring forth the roy - al di - a - dem, And crown him Lord of all.

Bring forth the roy - al di - a - dem, And crown him Lord of all.

388.

Hymn 346.—Lydia.—C. M.

Come, let us, who in Christ be - lieve, Our com - mon

Lydia.—*Continued.*

Sa - viour praise, To him with joy - ful voi - ces give The

glo - ry of his grace, The glo - ry of his grace.

389.

Hymn 389.—Mear.—C. M.

Try us, O God, and search the ground Of ev - 'ry sin - ful heart;

Whate'er of sin in us is found, O bid it all de - part!

390.   **Hymn 561.—Ortonville.—C M.**   *Dr Hastings.*

Let him to whom we now be-long His sov-'reign right as-sert, And take up ev-'ry thank-ful song, And ev-ry lov-ing heart, And ev-ry lov-ing heart.

391.   **Hymn 184.—St Martin's.—C M.**   *Tansur.*

Come, Holy Spi-rit, heaven-ly Dove, With all thy

St. Martin's.—*Continued*

quick'n - ing powers; Kin - dle a flame ol

sa - cred love In these cold hearts of ours,

---

392.   Hymn 819.—Siloam.—C. M.   *Woodbury.*

By cool Si - lo - am's sha - dy rill How sweet the li - ly grows!

How sweet the breath, be - neath the hill, Of Sha - ron's dew - y rose!

393. Hymn 15.—Reuben.—S. M.

Father, in whom we live, In whom we are, and move, In whom we are and move,

The glory, pow'r, and praise receive, The glory, pow'r, and praise receive, Of thy cre - ating love.

394. Hymn 613.—Admah.—6-8s.

Leader of faith - ful souls, and Guide Of all who trav - el to the sky.

Come, and with us, even us a - bide, Who would on thee a - lone re - ly;

Admah.—Continued

On thee a-lone our spi rits stay, While held in life's un ev en way.

395. Hymn 75.—Madrid.—6-8s. W Matthews

Mes - si - ah, joy of ev - 'ry heart Thou, thou the King of Glory art!

The Father's ev - er - last - ing Son! Thee it de - lights thy church to own;

For all our hopes on thee de - pend, Whose glorious mer - cies nev - er end.

396. Hymn 122.—Lennox.—6.6, 6.6. 8.8.

A - rise, my soul, a - rise! Shake off thy guil - ty fears; The bleeding Sac - ri -

- fice in my be - half ap - pears; Be - fore the throne my Sure - ty stands, My

name is writ - ten on his hands, My name is writ - ten on his hands.

---

397 Hymn 160.—Toplady.—6-7s.

Rock of A - ges cleft for me, Let me hide my - self in thee;

Let the wa - ter and the blood, From thy wound - ed side which flow'd,

Be of sin the doub - le cure, Save from wrath and make me pure.

398. Hymn 117.—**Martyn.**—8-7s.

{ Je - sus lov - er of my soul, Let me to thy bo - som fly, }
{ While the near - er wa - ters roll, While the tem - pest still is high: }
D. C. Safe in - to the hav - en guide, O receive my soul at last!

Hide me, O my Saviour, hide, Till the storm of life be past; *D. C.*

Hymn 738.—Watchman.—8-7s.

Dr. Mason.

Watchman, tell us of the night, What its signs of pro - mise are;

Traveller, o'er yon mountain's height See that glo - ry - beaming star!

Watchman, does its beauteous ray Aught of hope or joy foretell?

Traveller, yes; it brings the day, Promis'd day of Is - ra - el.

PRAYER MEETING AND SOCIAL SERVICE.

400.   Hymn 242.—Cleansing Fountain.—C. M.

There is a fountain fill'd with blood, Drawn from Im - man - uel's veins;

And sin - ners, plung'd be - neath that flood, Lose all their guil - ty stains.

Lose all their guil - ty stains, Lose all their guil - ty stains,

And sin - ners plung'd be - neath that flood, Lose all their guil - ty stains.

401.

Hymn 210.—"Come, ye Sinners."—8s and 7s.

Come, ye sin - ners, poor and wretch - ed, Weak and
Je - sus rea - dy stands to save you, Full of
D.C. Glo - ry, hon - our, and sal - va - tion, Christ the

FINE.   CHORUS.

wound - ed, sick, and sore; }
pi - ty, love, and pow'r; }   Turn to the Lord, and
Lord is come to reign.

D.C.

seek sal - va - tion, Sound the praise of his dear name:

402.

Hymn 256.—"Even Me."—8.7, 8.7, 3.   *W. B. Bradbury.*

Lord, I hear of showers of blessing Thou art scatt'ring full and free—
Showers, the thirsty land re - freshing; Let some drops now fall on me—

[278]

Ev - en me, Ev - en me, Let some drops now fall on me.

403. Hymn 763.—"Going Home." *Rev. W. McDonald.*

{ My heavenly home is bright and fair, Nor pain nor
{ Its glitt'ring tow'rs the sun out - shine, That heavenly

death can en - ter there } { I'm go - ing home, I'm go - ing
man - sion shall be mine } { To die no more, To die no

home, I'm go - ing home to die no more ; }
more, I'm go - ing home to die no more. }

[273]

404.   Hymn 525.—Cleansing.—S. M.

Fa - ther I dare be - lieve Thee mer - ci - ful and true; Thou wilt my guilty

soul forgive, My fal - len soul re - new. CHORUS. I am coming, Lord!

Coming now to thee! Wash me, cleanse me in the blood That flow'd on Cal - va - ry.

405.   Hymn 243.—"I am Trusting, Lord, in Thee."   *W. G. Fischer.*

Depth of mer - cy can there be Mer - cy still reserv'd for me?
CHORUS. D.C. I am trust - ing Lord in thee, Dear Lamb of Cal - va - ry;

[280]

"I am Trusting, Lord, in Thee."—*Continued*

Can my   God   his wrath for - bear? Me, the   chief of sin - ners spare? *D.C.*
Humbly   at   thy cross I   bow; Save me,   Je - sus, save me   now.

406.   **Hymn 781.—"I Need Thee Every Hour."**   *R. Lowry.*

I   need thee ev - 'ry hour, Most   gra - cious Lord; No ten - der voice like

thine Can   peace af - ford.   I   need thee, O I   need thee;

REFRAIN.

Every hour I   need thee; O bless me now, my   Saviour, I   come   to   thee!

[281]

407. **Hymn 780.—"One More Day's Work for Jesus."** *R. Lowry.*

One more day's work for Je - sus, One less of life for me!

But heav'n is near - er, And Christ is dear - er Than yes - ter - day, to me;

CHORUS.

His love and light Fill all my soul to - night. One more day's work for Je - sus,

One more day's work for Jesus, One more day's work for Jesus, One less of life for me.

[296]

Hymn 829.—"Safe in the Arms of Jesus." W. H. Doane.

CHORUS.

Safe in the arms of Je - sus, Safe on his gen - tle breast,
Safe in the arms of Je - sus, Safe on his gen - tle breast,

There by his love o'er - shad - ed, Sweet - ly my soul shall rest.
There by his love o'er - shad - ed, Sweet - ly my soul shall rest.

Hark ! 'tis the voice of an - gels, Borne in a song to me,

O - ver the fields of glo - ry, O - ver the jas - per sea.

D. C. for Chorus.

Hymn 352.—Meditation.

Freeman Lewis.

O how hap - py are they, Who the Saviour obey, And have laid up their treasure above!

Tongue can never express The sweet comfort and peace Of a soul in its ear - li - est love.

Hymn 834.—" Saviour, Like a Shepherd."

Saviour, like a Shepherd lead us, Much we need thy tend'rest care;
In thy pleasant pastures feed us, For our use thy fields pre - pare:

Blessed Je - sus, Blessed Je - sus, Thou hast bought us, thine we are,

Blessed Je - sus. Blessed Je - sus, Thou hast bought us, Thine we are.

411.   Hymn 838.—The Child's Desire.

I think, when I read that sweet sto - ry of old, When Je - sus was

here among men, How he call'd lit - tle chil - dren as

lambs to his fold, I should liked to have been with him then.

[285]

Hymn 774.—The Precious Name.

W. H. Doane.

Take the name of Je - sus with you, Child of sor - row and of woe;

It will joy and comfort give you, Take it, then, where'er you go.

CHORUS.

Precious name,   O how sweet,   Hope of earth and joy of heav'n.
Precious name,   O how sweet,

Precious name,   O how sweet - - - - Hope of earth and joy of heav'n.
Precious name, O how sweet, how sweet.

Hymn 760.—Unity.

Lowell Mason.

When shall we meet a - gain, Meet ne'er to sev - er?

When shall peace wreathe her chain round us for ev - er?

Our hearts will ne'er re - pose, Safe from each blast that blows,

In this dark vale of woes, Nev - er— no, nev - er!

Hymn 438.—The Pilgrim's Mission.

Philip Phillips.

Listen! the Master be - seech - eth, Calling each one by his name; His

voice to each loving heart reacheth, Its cheerfullest service to claim.

Go where the vineyard de - mand - eth Vinedresser's nurture and care; Or

go where the white harvest stand - eth, The joy of the reaper to share.

CHORUS.

Then work, brothers, work, let us slum - ber no long - er,

For God's call to la - bour grows strong - er and strong - er;

The light of this life shall be dark - en'd full soon,

Rit. . . . .

But the light of the bet - ter life rest - eth at noon.

T

[289]

Hymn 837.—Wilt Thou Hear the Voice of Praise?

Rev. J. Black.

Wilt thou hear the voice of praise Which the lit - tle chil - dren raise,

Thou who art, from end - less days, Glorious God of all?

While the circling year has sped, Thou hast heavenly bless - ings shed,

Like the dew, up - on each head; Still on thee we call.

416. Hymn 773.—**What a Friend we have in Jesus.** *C. C. Converse.*

What a friend we have in Je - sus, All our sins and griefs to bear!

What a pri - vi - lege to car - ry Ev - 'rything to God in pray'r!

O what peace we of - ten for - feit, O what needless pain we bear,

All because we do not car - ry Ev - 'rything to God in pray'r!

417. Hymn 782.—"**Work, for the Night is Coming.**" *Dr. Mason.*

Work for the night is com - ing, Work thro' the morn - ing hours;

Work while the dew is spark - ling, Work 'mid springing flowers;

Work when the day grows bright - er, Work in the glow - ing sun;

Work for the night is com - ing, When man's work is done.

www.ingramcontent.com/pod-product-compliance
Lightning Source LLC
Chambersburg PA
CBHW020501270326
41926CB00008B/697